WRITE YOUR OWN LIVING WILL

"A Living Will can protect you and your family from the i[...]ity, heartbreak, and financial devastation that your protracted death may mean."

—*U.S. News & World Report*

"A Living Will can unite a family whose members might otherwise have different interpretations about how an ill member of the family really feels about death—and it can help a doctor make a decision."

—Monroe T. Gilmour, M.D., Board Member,
American Association of Retired Persons (AARP)

"For people who are worried that they may someday be kept alive in a vegetative condition against their wishes—and at potentially enormous cost—a Living Will is essential, say lawyers, doctors and others who counsel individuals and their families on patients' rights."

—*Wall Street Journal*

"[My father] wanted to be remembered alive, aware, smiling at me, not as just a body connected to life-support systems. His Living Will was the last and best gift he gave me. All my memories are good. He lived the way he wanted and died the way he chose."

—"My Father's Best Gift," *Reader's Digest*

"No one can afford not to have some form of a Living Will."

—*Health Magazine*

"The Cruzan decision underscores the now prevailing opinion among medical groups that all adults should draw up Living Wills."

—*U.S. News & World Report*

———————————————

"Living Will statutes vary, so it's a good idea to sign a directive that complies with the law in your state. *You don't need a lawyer for this.*"

—*Business Week*

———————————————

"In the 1990 Cruzan case, the United States Supreme Court said it would honor Living Wills as proof of a patient's desire to end certain forms of medical care."

—*Pittsburgh Press*

———————————————

"While individual lawyers can also help with a Living Will, some of them say it probably isn't necessary to spend the money, since the forms are designed to be used without legal assistance."

—*Wall Street Journal*

———————————————

"Everyone, even young people, should make their wishes known to their families, friends and doctors."

—*Newsweek,* on Living Wills

———————————————

"Everyone age 21 or older should consider drafting a Living Will."

—*Money Magazine*

Write Your Own Living Will

Bradley E. Smith,
Attorney-at-Law
with
Jess M. Brallier

Crown Publishers, Inc.
New York

Published by Crown Publishers, Inc., 201 East 50th Street, New York, New York 10022. Member of the Crown Publishing Group.

Crown is a trademark of Crown Publishers, Inc.

Manufactured in the United States of America

Library of Congress Cataloging-in-Publication Data

Smith, Bradley E., 1956-
    Write your own living will / Bradley E. Smith with Jess M.
Brallier. — 1st ed.
        p.   cm.
    Includes index.
    1. Right to die—Law and legislation—United States—Popular
works. 2. Right to die—Law and legislation—United States—States—
Forms. I. Brallier, Jess M. II. Title.
KF3827.E87S63   1991
344.73'04197—dc20
[347.3044197]   90-27205
                                                 CIP

ISBN 0-517-58466-2

10 9 8 7 6 5 4 3 2 1

First Edition

CONTENTS

A NOTE TO THE READER

This book is designed to help you draft your own Living Will without the aid of an attorney. It is not intended as a substitute for professional legal advice. If you have any doubts or questions about legal matters not answered by this book, you should consult an attorney.

The guidelines and forms included in this book are current as of the date of publication. However, this area of the law is evolving and state statutes covering Living Wills are always subject to change. To be certain your particular Living Will conforms to the most recent guidelines issued by your state, you can have it reviewed by an attorney. Also, this book's state-by-state guide includes telephone listings for state agencies that deal with patients' rights. You can call your own agency to inquire about any changes in state Living Will guidelines.

Be sure to read the entire book carefully before you attempt to complete your Living Will form.

WRITE YOUR
OWN
LIVING WILL

INTRODUCTION

"Life is not simple, nor is death."
—Anonymous

A Living Will is a document that indicates your wish not to be kept alive by artificial means or heroic measures if you are suffering from a terminal condition and your death is imminent.

Although the form of a Living Will may vary slightly from state to state, it generally directs your physician and medical care facility to withhold or withdraw life-sustaining procedures, permitting a natural and dignified death.

Until quite recently, death was a private matter that occurred in your home, with only your family in attendance. But now, at the end of the twentieth century, your death will most likely occur in a hospital or nursing home (as 80 percent of all deaths in the United States do). Advanced medical care and technology now present us all with difficult choices regarding our care and treatment as death approaches.

Over the last twenty years, as death has become more institutionalized, extraordinary advances in medical science have enabled physicians to extend life long beyond your ability to see, hear, speak, or even think. Many people have come to feel that such artificial extension of life would merely prolong suffering for both them and their families. This has been the impetus for so-called "right to die" movements, which have forced state legislatures and the courts to address these difficult issues.

In 1976, the hearts of all Americans were touched when we learned that the parents of Karen Ann Quinlan, a young woman in a PVS (Persistent Vegetative State), could not remove their daughter's respirator and let her die naturally. To do what they were sure Karen would want, the Quinlans had to overcome an expensive, draining, prolonged, and uncertain fight in the courts. The Quinlan case was the first to challenge profoundly the manner in which we view death, medical treatment, and technology.

Because of the Quinlan case we realized at last that medical technology could produce a previously unknown hell between the life we enjoy and the death we anticipate.

Within a decade of the Quinlan case, the courts, on a state-by-state basis, established a consensus:

The choice of the individual patient would in most cases be respected, even after that individual has become incapable of expressing that choice.

It followed, then, that there should be a mechanism that allowed you to make your choice known, while still mentally capable of doing so. The choice would have to be legally enforceable. Such laws would have to be conceived so that your doctor and hospital would be free from any civil and criminal liability that might result from their following your direction.

By the end of the 1980s, most states had responded to this demand by enacting statutes that give legal recognition to what is clearly the most important product of these efforts, the Living Will—*a document that indicates your wish not to be kept alive by artificial means or heroic measures if you are suffering from a terminal condition and your death is imminent.*

A substantial majority of the American people endorse the basic principle of the Living Will. In a recent Gallup poll, 81 percent favored withholding life-support systems from competent and incompetent terminally ill patients, *if they so direct.* In addition, 85

1

percent agreed with the statement, "A patient with a terminal disease ought to be able to tell his doctor to let him die rather than to extend his life when no cure is in sight."

According to the American Medical Association, up to 20 percent of adult Americans have written a Living Will. Research indicates that people complete a Living Will for three key reasons:

1) the desire to maintain control over their medical care when they may not be able to communicate their wishes;
2) to free those they love most—spouse, parents, children—from the need to make heart-rending decisions at a time when emotions are likely to overwhelm rational judgment; and
3) to avoid the financial devastation and the many hardships that result from artifically prolonged life.

Legal support for the public consensus was provided by the United States Supreme Court in the case of Nancy Cruzan, decided in 1990. A majority of the justices agreed that an individual may have a constitutional right to refuse medical treatment and endorsed the concept of a Living Will as a method for clearly defining the wishes of an individual to exercise that right.

Even more recently, in November 1990, the U.S. Congress enacted the Patient Self-Determination Act, which will, by 1992, require hospitals, health maintenance organizations (HMOs), nursing facilities, and home health care providers to advise patients of their rights to make health care decisions in advance with advance directives such as Living Wills.

The publication of this book is, in great part, a response to the public's demand for a readily available, simplified guide to writing a Living Will. If you do not determine your own care through a Living Will, your family may face a no-win situation: as long as they must guess your intentions, guilt will remain whether they permit your suffering to continue or try to end it. A Living Will can free them from this horrible burden.

AT RISK

As we begin the 1990s, more Americans recognize that a dilemma such as the one faced by Karen Ann Quinlan's family is not an isolated case. There are thousands of patients in comas or suffering from terminal conditions. The patients could include the college student pulled from a violent auto accident or the young mother with cancer. Or they could include your spouse, your parents, or your children—even you.

Imagine being in a coma.

Imagine that you cannot talk or move (and never will again).

Imagine not having any control over the extent and cost of your medical care.

Imagine your loving family breaking apart, fighting bitterly with each other, trying to guess what your wishes might be.

Imagine that everything you had hoped to leave to your spouse and family is lost, gone to pay for life support you never wanted.

It can happen.

Irene

Irene lies in a hospital, dying, drifting in and out of consciousness. Her pain is obvious.

Irene's skin is now gray; it hangs from her bones. She has not felt the sun for two years. Nasogastric tubes feed her. Other tubes drain her wastes. A respirator breathes for her.

Irene will not recover.

In the 1940s, Irene danced at Radio City Music Hall. Soldiers heading home through New York City admired her talent and beauty. She left dancing when she married the best-looking soldier of all. They raised four children and lived fully the life they first dreamed of in the coffee shop behind Radio City. But then Irene's husband suddenly died, just a month before Irene's cancer was discovered.

Because her cancer worsened and her periods of consciousness decreased, her children begged that her respirator be disconnected so that she could die peacefully.

The hospital refused.

Irene's heart monitoring machine beeps to remind—perhaps convince—her children that Irene is "alive." Irene will continue to suffer, as will her children. The cost of keeping Irene alive continues to mount at a rate of thousands of dollars per week. All the money the handsome soldier and his dancing wife saved for forty years disappeared in just four months.

William

William, a forty-five-year-old executive, was being driven home by a coworker after an uneventful workday. William unhitched his seat belt to reach for his raincoat in the backseat, another car suddenly pulled out, his friend braked, the car skidded into a tree, and William's head slammed into the side post and windshield. An hour later, William was in a coma.

Four months later, a still comatose William developed pneumonia. Because William did not have a Living Will, his wife was asked to decide whether to withhold treatment and let him die, or agree to the administration of powerful antibiotics and mechanical ventilation.

The attending physician vividly recalls William's wife's anguish: "I don't know what to do! We never thought this could happen. Not to us. I don't know what's right!"

Mary

In 1990, Mary turned thirty-two. Since an auto accident on an icy night seven years ago, she's done nothing. For seven years she hasn't smiled or laughed, or even cried. For seven years she hasn't held a hand, smelled spring or fall, or seen a snow-

fall. For seven years she's not said a word. Mary has lain so still for so long that her hands have curled into claws, and nurses jam napkins under her fingers to keep the nails from cutting her palms.

Her parents are convinced that Mary would not want to go on this way: "She would hate being like this." They "know" Mary would want her feeding tube disconnected, "for mercy's sake . . . those were her wishes."

Mary's state has a Living Will law that permits such wishes to be fulfilled . . . but Mary never put those wishes in writing.

It is likely that Mary will "live" the next thirty years as she has the last seven.

Skip

Among the awards and trophies honoring both his academic and athletic accomplishments is a photo of "Skip Jones, Homecoming King." Next to it is another photo, the one used in the newspapers when he was selected to the All-Conference football team. Only thirteen months after being so honored, Skip was first laid onto the bed below the neatly placed awards and photos. Skip has now lain there, in a fetal position, for eleven years. His open mouth constantly twists and contorts from one hideous grimace to the next. His wrists stiffly bend down, his fingers curl upward, his legs pull in tight against his chest. A plastic tube runs between the bedside air compressor and the tracheotomy connection surgically implanted in Skip's throat. Another plastic tube feeds a liquid lunch through a surgical incision in Skip's stomach, and yet another tube simultaneously empties what remains of his breakfast.

In September 1979, nineteen-year-old Skip Jones underwent a "simple procedure" at a hospital. Something went wrong. Skip's heart stopped during the operation. He suffered massive brain damage from lack of oxygen to the brain. Although clinically alive, the Skip that his parents, fiancée, nephews, and nieces loved so much was gone. All of Skip's brain functions were destroyed. He no longer could taste or touch. He no longer could love or receive love. No pleasure of any sort was possible. He was, essentially, a vegetable, and he would remain so for over ten years.

Because Skip had not prepared a Living Will, Skip's doctors would not discontinue his treatment. Skip's family asked the courts for help. Although his parents, other family members, and Skip's best friends all testified that he had been horrified by the reports of Karen Ann Quinlan's plight, and although they all testified that Skip had said on numerous occasions he would never want his life artifically sustained, there was no written proof of Skip's wishes.

Skip continues to live his hell.

Nellie

Nellie, mother of three, is being fed through a tube inserted in her nose. She lies on her back in a nursing home bed.

After five years of visits to the nursing home, her children no longer come. They say, tearfully, that they can no longer live their own lives and watch "what remains of Mom." Their personal and professional lives have suffered from their draining sessions with their mother.

Because she tries to pull the tube out of her nose, Nellie's hands are now tied to the bed rails. Even with her hands tied, Nellie keeps trying to pull the tube out of her nose. As she struggles, her bedding slips to the floor. Mom, helpless, lies shamefully naked in the cold of the stark room.

An hour passes before another patient covers Nellie's bare body. Then he pauses. Perhaps remembering his own mother or wife, or even thinking of himself, he begins to weep.

REAL COSTS

The Gallaghers

Mike and Betty Gallagher looked forward to their retirement, planning to live on Social Security and Mike's pension. But at sixty-eight, in the year of his retirement, Mike's health suddenly worsened. Soon he was confused and needed help just to eat and walk. In 1982, exactly two years from the day he retired, Mike entered a nursing home. Two years later, after a series of illnesses, Mike was mentally incompetent and being kept alive by a respirator. It was only when Betty and her children asked that the respirator be disconnected—as they knew Mike would have wanted—did Betty learn that without a Living Will Mike's wishes could not be fulfilled.

By the time Mike died in 1989, the Gallaghers, despite a lifetime of work and the security of a pension, had sunk into poverty.

Mike's first year in the nursing home cost $14,000—$5,000 more than the Gallaghers' total income. Because the Gallaghers had $8,000 in savings, $2,000 in life insurance cash value, $5,000 in U.S. Savings Bonds, and $300 in a Christmas Club savings plan, they were "too rich" to qualify for their state's Medicaid program.

The only way Betty could keep Mike in a nursing home was to become impoverished. Medicaid pays the bills only after the family assets and income run out.

It took Betty only six months to spend on nursing home care what they had saved in forty-two years of marriage.

You will probably die in a hospital or nursing home—eight out of ten Americans do.

Hospitals and nursing homes are legally bound to keep you alive by artifical means or heroic measures even if you are suffering from a terminal condition and your death is imminent. If you enter these institutions without specific written instructions (that is, a Living Will), you risk an artificial extension of "life," a prolonged existence that quickly drains your family's emotional and financial resources.

Such an existence may cost your family a fortune and put them at financial risk for years to come. Across America, the average billing for a hospitalized terminal patient maintained on life support is about **$850 per day.*** After a week, total costs would be **$6,000;** for a month, **$26,000;** and after only one year, **$310,000.**

You and your family will not escape potential financial ruin by turning to a nursing home. There, the average length of stay is 456 days—**but Medicare pays for only 100 days.** Half of all nursing home expenses are paid out of pocket by patients and their families. **On average, only thirteen weeks elapse from the time a patient enters a nursing home until the spouse left at home is impoverished.**†

Medical costs are soaring. The cost of long-term life-support care for terminal patients is soaring even higher. Look at these potential costs:

- Maintenance of a patient on a respirator may cost as much as **an additional $850 a day** beyond a hospital's regular daily rate.‡
- The average **daily** cost for an elderly stroke victim in a hospital's intensive care unit is over **$1,000.**
- In the United States, **$40 billion a year** goes for nursing home care; **52 percent** of that is paid out of pocket by patients and their families (42 percent by Medicaid, 2 percent by Medicare, 1 percent by private insurance, and 3 percent from other sources).†
- Throughout the United States, a year's stay in a nursing home averages **$30,000**†; (the costs do vary

---

SOURCE: **U.S. News & World Report*, July 20, 1987.
†*Consumer Reports*, May 1988.
‡*Modern Maturity*, June–July 1988.

from facility to facility and from state to state. For example, one typical nursing home in Connecticut charges families $165 per day, or **$60,225 a year**§).

- In just the next ten years, the costs of a year's stay in a nursing home will jump to about **$70,000.**†
- In most cases, **insurance does not completely cover the cost** of a nursing home.*
- About two-thirds of all residents who enter a nursing home end up on Medicaid by "spending down" their income and assets until they become eligible for coverage.*

- To qualify for Medicaid coverage, an elderly person must have no more than $1,800 in individual assets and virtually all income, such as pensions, must be applied to the nursing home bill.*

Can you afford *not* to have a Living Will?

SOURCE: *U.S. News & World Report*, July 20, 1987.
†*Consumer Reports*, May 1988.
§Private hospital in-house confidential memo.

WHAT A LIVING WILL IS

What is a Living Will?

Simply stated, a Living Will is a document that indicates your wish not to be kept alive by artificial means or heroic measures if you are suffering from a terminal condition and your death is imminent.

Although the form of a Living Will may vary slightly from state to state, it generally directs your physician and medical care facility to withhold or withdraw life-sustaining procedures, permitting a natural and dignified death.

A Living Will may also be referred to as a "Medical Directive," "Natural Death Declaration," or "Life-Support System Affidavit." All describe the same basic document.

What is a "terminal condition," for purposes of a Living Will?

Both state legislatures and the courts have struggled with defining this term in a precise and accurate way without being unduly restrictive. It is generally agreed that regardless of legal definition, the ultimate determination of a terminal state must lie within the attending physician's professional discretion.

The Uniform Rights of the Terminally Ill Act (1989) defines "terminal condition" as "an incurable and irreversible condition that, without the administration of life-sustaining treatment, will, in the opinion of the attending physician, result in death within a relatively short time." Most states have interpreted the term in similar language.

I'm unsure of what "life-sustaining" or "life-prolonging" treatments and procedures mean. How do I determine what treatments I might want or not want?

These terms, "life-sustaining" and "life-prolonging," which are frequently found in Living Will statutes, are not consistently interpreted from state to state. Your physician can best provide assistance in defining these terms. The Checklist of Medical Interventions on page 33 should be used as a guide for such a consultation.

What purpose does a Living Will serve?

A Living Will ensures that your wishes about medical treatment will be respected even at a time when you may be unable to express them.

Equally important, a Living Will relieves your family of the burden of making an agonizing life or death decision regarding your prolonged medical treatment, should you become incompetent or unable to communicate. The Living Will is a written set of instructions to your loved ones and doctors that eliminates the need for family members to guess about your intentions, should you become terminally ill.

What are the views of the major religious denominations in America regarding Living Wills?

The attitudes of the major denominations toward Living Wills generally reflect the opinions of the American public. For example, leading representatives of the Roman Catholic Church, United Church of Christ, the Central Conference of American Rabbis, the Presbytery of New York City, and the United Methodist Church have all spoken out in favor of a patient's right to a natural and dignified death.

If you have further questions, consult your priest, minister, or rabbi.

What is the difference between a Living Will and a Last Will and Testament? Do I need to have a Living Will if I already have a Last Will and Testament?

You need a Living Will *whether or not* you have made a Last Will and Testament.

The Living Will is a completely different document from your Last Will and Testament. A Living Will is meant to be activated during your lifetime if the need arises. It deals only with medical treatment issues, not matters of property.

A Last Will and Testament provides for the disposition of your *assets, after* your death. It has no binding legal effect prior to that time.

What is the difference between a Living Will and a "living trust"?

Like a Last Will and Testament, the "living trust" is a document that addresses disposition and investment of various types of property and income. A "living trust" takes effect while an individual is competent and generally is used to minimize probate expenses and estate and inheritance taxes.

Does everyone need a Living Will?

Anyone over the age of 18, who wants to spare his or her family the anguish and ruinous expense of extended care for a terminally ill, suffering patient should have a Living Will. If you prefer a dignified death to a life sustained only by respirators, feeding tubes, and powerful drugs, you should have a Living Will.

WRITING YOUR LIVING WILL

Is a lawyer necessary to prepare a Living Will?

No. Just as with a Last Will and Testament, the Living Will does not *require* the services of an attorney so long as the document follows the proper formalities. For your convenience, this book includes preprinted Living Will forms that you can fill out in a few minutes. However, if properly drafted, signed, and witnessed, even a handwritten Living Will will be given full force and effect.

As we have said before, this is an evolving area of law and state statues are subject to change. If you want to confirm that your Living Will conforms to the most recent legislation, you may want to consult an attorney. It is certainly advisable to consult an attorney if you have legal questions not addressed by this lay guide to the Living Will.

What if my state has no Living Will statute?

You may still execute a Living Will, using the general form (Form #1) provided in this book on page 37. This form is a hybrid of the provisions most generally found in Living Will statutes and should be accepted by the courts in your state as persuasive evidence of your intentions.

You should nonetheless discuss your decision to make a Living Will with your family and your physician to ensure that your wishes will be honored.

Note: When meeting with your physician, be sure to discuss the items on the Checklist of Medical Interventions (page 33).

How old must I be to have a Living Will? Do I have to be 18? Can a parent or guardian do a Living Will for a minor?

There are slight variations among the states on the age you must be to execute a Living Will. You should consult the state-by-state guide (Chapter 8) in this book.

Similarily, a few states provide for issuance of a medical directive by a parent or legal guardian of a minor in a terminal condition. These provisions are noted in the state-by-state guide.

Who should be a witness to my Living Will?

It is essential that you consult this book's state-by-state guide (Chapter 8) before executing your Living Will, as there are a number of variations on witness requirements among the states.

Generally, a witness should be over 18 years of age, unrelated by blood or marriage to you, not potentially entitled to any portion of your estate either by will or operation of law, nor financially responsible for your medical care.

No attending physician or his or her employee, or any employee of the health facility in which you may be a patient should act as a witness.

If you are a patient in a hospital or nursing care facility at the time of execution of the Living Will, many states require that a state-qualified ombudsman or patient advocate either be present or act as a witness.

Again, be sure to follow the state requirements for witnessing to ensure the enforceability of your Living Will.

If I split my time between two states (for example, if I winter in the South and summer in the North), does it matter in which state I execute my Living Will?

In this case, you should execute two Living Wills, meeting the statutory requirements of each state. This will ensure that your intentions are expressed with the appropriate formalities, regardless of where you are residing.

Where should I keep my Living Will?

The Living Will should be in a location known to and accessible to close family members in the event of an emergency. It should *not* be kept in a safe deposit box to which you have the only access.

In addition, a copy should be given to your treating physician who, after reviewing the provisions with you, should place it in your medical file with the Checklist of Medical Interventions (page 33). (Many states *require* that you give a copy to your attending physician—otherwise he or she may not become aware of its existence.)

You may also want to leave a copy with your clergyman.

NOTE: This book includes a Living Will Record where you can note who has received copies of your Living Will. It is not legally necessary to complete this form. However, it is convenient to do so for whenever you might wish to revoke, change, or renew your Living Will declaration.

REVOKING OR CHANGING YOUR LIVING WILL

May I revoke my Living Will?

Absolutely yes. Your Living Will may be revoked at any time by you, without regard to your mental or physical condition. Your revocation may be done in writing (signed and dated by you), orally, by defacement or destruction of the Living Will, or by a physical sign communicating your intention to revoke. Your revocation should be communicated to your attending physican to be effective.

In addition, several state statutes provide that you must re-execute your Living Will or it will automatically expire. If your state is one that requires re-execution, this requirement and the timing of the re-execution will be noted in the state-by-state guide in Chapter 8.

Can someone else have my Living Will revoked even if I do not want it revoked?

A properly completed, signed, and notarized Living Will is a legal document. It can only be revoked by you or by someone acting at your direction.

If you wish to have someone revoke it *for you*, you should consult the state-by-state guide (Chapter 8) for requirements specific to your state.

If I change physicians, should I change my Living Will?

If you change physicians, your medical records containing a copy of your Living Will and your Checklist of Medical Interventions (page 33) will normally be transferred to the new doctor. However, you should review the provisions of your Living Will with your new physician to ensure that he or she understands your wishes.

What happens if I change physicians and forget to notify my new physician of my Living Will?

In this case, it would be up to your family to provide the physician with a copy of your Living Will, should you be unable to communicate.

WHEN YOUR INSTRUCTIONS BECOME EFFECTIVE

Under what circumstances does a Living Will become effective?

A Living Will declaration becomes effective when it is communicated to your attending physician and you are determined by that physician, often with the concurrence of another examining physician, to be in a terminal condition and no longer able to make or to communicate decisions regarding the administration of life-sustaining treatment. If the requests made in your Living Will are reasonable and lawful under normal medical practice—as they will be if the instructions and forms in this book are followed and used correctly—your health care providers will generally proceed to carry them out.

If, for example, I live in Connecticut, execute a Living Will there, and am hospitalized in North Carolina after a serious accident, will my Connecticut Living Will be effective in North Carolina?

To the extent that your Living Will is valid and legally executed in Connecticut, it will likely be effective in another state, at least to the extent of creating a strong presumption of your wishes to reject certain types of life-sustaining treatment.

However, unless there is some uniform law adopted by *all* the states, problems with specific enforcement of Living Wills from one state to another may be encountered. Still, the likelihood of your wishes being honored is far greater if you have made a Living Will, even in a different state, than if you have no Living Will at all.

What if my physician refuses to honor the provisions of my Living Will?

In most states, a treating physician who, for reasons of conscience or otherwise, refuses to carry out the directives of a patient's Living Will is under an obligation to transfer care to another physician who will honor the patient's wishes.

In several states, such a refusal is deemed to be unprofessional conduct and may even expose the physician to a civil penalty.

Must my doctor and/or family honor the instructions given in my Living Will? What if my family disagrees with my decision?

The recent "right-to-die" case decided by the United States Supreme Court (*Cruzan v. State of Missouri*, in which the family of Nancy Cruzan, a thirty-two-year-old woman in a persistent vegetative state, wished to remove life support) suggested that Living Wills are valuable tools to assist judges in making difficult rulings on artificially prolonging life. Our courts, both federal and state, have taken varying views on the legal enforceability of Living Wills, but all accord them considerable weight if they are in the proper form and duly executed, regardless of any contrary wishes of a family member.

If there is a dispute over the expectation of a patient's recovery between medical experts, in all likelihood the Living Will would not be enforced, as the legal presumption must always be in favor of preserving human life.

We recommend that you discuss the instructions contained in your Living Will with both your family and physician. This increases the likelihood that your Living Will directives will be honored.

OTHER COMMON QUESTIONS

What if I wish to donate my organs? Does a Living Will affect that choice?

The Living Will is a natural complement to an organ donation designation. In fact, organs from a Living Will donor are likely to be more useful than those from a patient who dies following a long period of artificially sustained life. However, you can make a Living Will regardless of whether you designate yourself as an organ donor, and vice versa.

Organ donation cannot be considered until the donor is legally dead. *Although treatment can be terminated to comply with a Living Will, in <u>no</u> case can treatment be terminated for the purpose of making an organ donation.*

If I have a Living Will and I'm pregnant and go on life-support, perhaps because of a serious accident, what happens to my unborn child?

For situations involving pregnancy, most states mandate that a Living Will be ignored.

In other states, treatment will not be withheld or withdrawn from a pregnant woman so long as it is possible that the fetus will develop to the point of live birth with the continued application of life-sustaining treatment.

If this is of concern to you, you should consult with your obstetrician.

May I delegate my decision about my medical care to a relative? Or somebody else?

Generally, a Living Will expresses only *your* directions about medical care. However, some states' Living Will statutes provide for the designation of another to perform this function within the Living Will declaration. Also, many states have durable power of attorney or health care proxy laws, which allow an agent to make return medical decisions on your behalf.

We recommend that you very *carefully* consider giving such a right to another, even a relative, as the potential for conflict of interest and even abuse of that decision-making power is great. Remember, too, that part of the value of a Living Will is that it can *spare* your loved ones the agony of having to make decisions about your life and death.

If I don't have a Living Will, is there a presumption that I do want my life to be artificially prolonged indefinitely?

Many state Living Will statutes specifically address this question. Most say that not executing a Living Will creates no presumption one way or the other. However, if you have not expressed your opposition to life-sustaining treatments, it is likely that they will be applied.

What happens if I don't have a Living Will?

Without a clear expression of the patient's wishes, physicians and hospitals are generally duty-bound to continue life-support systems, regardless of cost.

If a Living Will has been executed, the medical care-givers have in hand the specific directive of the patient and, in most cases, will honor that directive.

Could a physician be subject to criminal or civil liability for terminating a patient's life-support system as directed by a Living Will?

Attending physicians and those under their authority and direction, as well as the facilities in which they work, are generally extended immunity from liability as long as reasonable medical judgment is exercised in following a Living Will's directives.

Would executing a Living Will cancel any life insurance policies I might have?

Both state statutes and public policy dictate that Living Wills cannot affect an individual's insurance contracts.

For example, the Uniform Rights of the Terminally Ill Act addresses this question with the following provision:

The making of a [Living Will] does not affect in any manner the sale, procurement, or issuance of any policy of life insurance or annuity, nor does it affect, impair, or modify the terms of an existing policy of life insurance or annuity. A policy of life insurance or annuity is not legally impaired or invalidated in any manner by the withholding or withdrawal of life-sustaining treatment from an insured qualified patient.

Similarily, it is not permissible to require the execution of a Living Will as a condition for obtaining any type of insurance policy.

Could my decision to have life-support systems withheld or withdrawn be considered suicide, invalidating my life insurance policies?

State statutes specifically provide that a directive to withhold medical treatment cannot be considered suicide, so your life insurance policies would not be affected by your Living Will.

Is my Living Will valid for a lifetime?

You should review your existing Living Will at least every two years and re-sign and redate it before filing it away.

It is a good idea to re-execute your Living Will every five years in the presence of a notary.

Because the laws in the various states continue to develop in this area, it is quite possible that changes will occur in the future that would require a redrafting of your Living Will. For this reason, the state-by-state guide (Chapter 8) includes a phone number for each state's public health department. The public health department can provide information regarding any possible revisions in your state's Living Will law. (Note, also, that each state's health department has been provided with a copy of this book.)

May I videotape my Living Will declaration?

Although some states provide a mechanism for executing a Last Will and Testament by videotape, as yet no provision has been made for Living Wills. It is possible that videotaping will become acceptable in the next ten years or so since a maker's wishes may sometimes be more clearly expressed through that medium. At the moment, however, your Living Will must be in written form.

STATE-BY-STATE GUIDE

There is no federal Living Will law.

At the time of publication, forty-three states and the District of Columbia had enacted some form of Living Will statute.

Although all of the state laws share certain characteristics, there are many variations. For this reason, a state-by-state guide is included here so that you can determine your state's precise requirements for validly executing your Living Will.

These summaries address only information required for execution and revocation of Living Wills. They are not complete summaries of the respective state statutes. If questions arise that are not covered by the summaries or addressed in the question-and-answer material (Chapters 3 through 7), the actual state statute should be consulted. For this reason, the title of the statute has been included. Additionally, all of the statutes discussed are subject to amendment or repeal, in whole or in part, by state legislation. The guide includes telephone listings for state agencies that deal with patients' rights; call them to inquire about any changes in your state's guidelines. If you are not certain that your Living Will conforms to the current legislation in your state, you can have it reviewed by an attorney.

NOTE: For those states without a Living Will law, we have provided guidelines derived from other Living Will statutes.

ALABAMA

Title of state's Living Will law: "Natural Death Act"
Department of Public Health: (205) 242-5052
Minimum age to have a Living Will: 19
Witness Requirements:
- Two or more
- 19 years or older
- Not related by blood or marriage
- No potential claim to declarant's estate, by will or operation of law
- Not directly financially responsible for medical care

Revocation Requirements:
- Physical destruction or defacement, or
- Written revocation by declarant or person acting at direction of declarant, or
- Oral revocation in presence of witness 19 or older who signs and dates a writing confirming the revocation

Filing Requirements: Responsibility of declarant to notify physician of Living Will for filing with medical records
Other: None

ALASKA

Title of state's Living Will law: "Rights of Terminally Ill Act"
Department of Health and Social Services: (907) 465-3030
Minimum age to have a Living Will: 18
Witness Requirements:
- Two, or one qualified to take acknowledgments under state law
- 18 years or older
- Not related by blood or marriage
- May not charge a fee

Revocation Requirements: At any time and in any manner declarant is able to communicate intent to revoke, regardless of mental or physical condition
Filing Requirements: Declarant must give copy to attending physician for inclusion in medical records
Other: None

ARIZONA

Title of state's Living Will law: "Medical Treatment Decision Act"
Department of Health Services: (602) 542-1024
Minimum age to have a Living Will: 18
Witness Requirements:
- Two adults
- Not related by blood or marriage
- No potential claim to declarant's estate, by will or operation of law
- Not directly financially responsible for medical treatment

Revocation Requirements:
- Physical destruction or defacement, or
- Written, signed, dated revocation of declarant, or
- Verbal revocation by declarant or person(s) to whom revocation is communicated

Filing Requirements: declarant must notify attending physician
Other: none

ARKANSAS

Title of state's Living Will law: "Arkansas Rights of the Terminally Ill or Permanently Unconscious Act"
Department of Health: (501) 661-2111
Minimum age to have a Living Will: 18
Witness Requirements: Two
Revocation Requirements: At any time and in any manner upon communication to attending physician or health care provider by declarant or witness to revocation
Filing Requirements: Must notify attending physician for filing with declarant's medical records
Other: Separate declarations for 1) patient in a terminal condition; and 2) patient who is permanently unconscious

CALIFORNIA

Title of state's Living Will law: "Natural Death Act"
Department of Health Services: (916) 445-1248
Minimum age to have a Living Will: 18
Witness Requirements:
- Two, not related by blood or marriage
- No potential claim to declarant's estate, by will or operation of law
- Not attending physician, employee of attending physician or health facility where declarant is a patient

- **NOTE:** Directive will have no effect if declarant is a patient in a skilled nursing facility at the time the directive is executed unless one of the two witnesses is a patient advocate or ombudsman as designated by the State Department of Aging.

Revocation Requirements:
- Physical destruction or defacement, or
- Signed, dated written revocation by declarant, or
- Verbal expression to attending physician by declarant or person acting on behalf of declarant

Filing Requirements: Declarant must give copy to attending physician to be filed with medical records
Other:
- **Re-execution Requirements: Automatic expiration after five years from date of execution, unless patient is comatose or incapable of communication with attending physician; directive is then effective for duration of comatose condition or until declarant is able to communicate intentions**

COLORADO

Title of state's Living Will law: "Colorado Medical Treatment Decision Act"
Department of Health: (303) 331-4600
Minimum age to have a Living Will: 18
Witness Requirements:
- Two adults
- No potential claim to declarant's estate, by will or operation of law
- Not a physician, or employee of the attending physician or health care facility in which declarant is a patient
- Not a patient or resident of any health care facility in which declarant is a patient

Revocation Requirements:
- Physical destruction or defacement, or
- Written revocation, or
- Oral revocation

Filing Requirements: Declarant or someone acting for the declarant must submit copy to attending physician for entry into medical records
Other: Provides procedure for challenging the validity of a declaration

CONNECTICUT

Title of state's Living Will law: "Removal of Life-Support Systems"

Department of Health Services: (203) 566-2038
Minimum age to have a Living Will: 18
Witness Requirements: Two
Revocation Requirements: None
Filing Requirements: None
Other: None

DELAWARE

Title of state's Living Will law: "Delaware Death with Dignity Act"
Division of Public Health: (302) 739-4701
Minimum age to have a Living Will: 18
Witness Requirements:
- No potential claim to declarant's estate, by will or operation of law
- No direct financial responsibility for declarant's medical care
- Not an employee of hospital or other health care facility in which declarant is a patient
- NOTE: **If declarant is a resident of a sanitarium, rest home, nursing home, boarding home, or related institution, one witness must be a patient advocate or ombudsman designated by the Division of Aging, or the state-appointed Public Guardian**

Revocation Requirements:
- Physical destruction or defacement, or
- Oral statement in presence of two persons over 18, or
- Written revocation signed and dated by declarant, or
- Executing a new declaration, expressing a contrary intent

Filing Requirements: Declarant must provide copy to hospital or attending physician for filing with medical records
Other: None

DISTRICT OF COLUMBIA

Title of state's Living Will law: "Natural Death Act"
Department of Human Services: (202) 673-7700
Minimum age to have a Living Will: 18
Witness Requirements:
- 18, unrelated by marriage or blood
- Not one who signed declaration on behalf of declarant
- No potential estate claim, by will or operation of law

- Not directly financially responsible for declarant's medical care
- Not attending physician or his employee or employee of health care facility in which declarant is a patient
- NOTE: **If declarant is a patient in an intermediate care or skilled care facility at time a declaration is executed, one witness must be a patient advocate or ombudsman**

Revocation Requirements:
- Physical destruction or defacement, or
- Written revocation signed and dated by declarant or one acting at direction of declarant (effective only when communicated to attending physician), or
- Verbal revocation in presence of witness 18 or over who signs and dates a written confirmation

Filing Requirements: Declarant responsible for notification of attending physician for filing with medical records
Other: None

FLORIDA

Title of state's Living Will law: "Life Prolonging Procedure Act of Florida"
Health and Rehabilitative Services: (904) 488-2381
Minimum age to have a Living Will: 18
Witness Requirements: Two, one of whom is neither a spouse nor blood relative
Revocation Requirements:
- Written revocation, signed and dated, or
- Physical cancellation or destruction, or
- Oral expression of intent to revoke

Filing Requirements: Declarant must notify attending physician
Other: None

GEORGIA

Title of state's Living Will law: "Living Wills"
Department of Human Resources: (404) 894-7505
Minimum age to have a Living Will: 18
Witness Requirements:
- Two adults, unrelated by blood or marriage
- No potential claim against declarant's estate
- Not attending physician or physician's employee
- Not an employee of hospital or skilled nursing facility in which declarant is a patient
- Not directly financially responsible for declarant's medical care

- NOTE: If declarant is patient in hospital or skilled nursing facility at the time Living Will is executed, it must be signed in presence of two qualified witnesses as well as either chief of the hospital medical staff or any physician on the medical staff who is not treating declarant, or the medical director or non-treating physician in a skilled nursing facility

Revocation Requirements:
- Physical destruction or defacement, or
- Written revocation, signed and dated, or
- Oral revocation

Filing Requirements: None

Other:
- **Re-execution Requirements: Automatic expiration after seven years from date of execution, unless patient is comatose or incapable of communication with attending physician; directive is then effective for duration of comatose condition or until declarant is able to communicate intentions**

HAWAII

Title of state's Living Will law: "Medical Treatment Decisions"
Department of Health: (808) 548-6505
Minimum age to have a Living Will: 18
Witness Requirements:
- Two or more, over 18
- Not related by blood, marriage, or adoption
- Not the attending physician, an employee of the attending physician, or an employee of the medical care facility in which the declarant is a patient

Revocation Requirements:
- Physical destruction or defacement, or
- Written revocation, signed and dated, to be recorded by physician, or
- Verbal revocation, in presence of two adult witnesses, to be recorded by physician

Filing Requirements: Declarant must provide copy of directive to physician to be filed with medical records

Other: No physician participating in decision to withhold or withdraw life-sustaining procedures from declarant may participate in transplanting any vital organs from declarant to another person

IDAHO

Title of state's Living Will law: "Natural Death Act"

Department of Health and Welfare: (208) 334-5700
Minimum age to have a Living Will: any emancipated minor or any person over 18
Witness Requirements:
- Two adults
- Not a health care provider or employee of a health care provider
- Not an operator or employee of a community care facility
- Not related by blood, marriage, or adoption
- No potential claim to declarant's estate, by will or operation of law

Revocation Requirements:
- Physical destruction or defacement, or
- Written, signed revocation by declarant, or
- Verbal revocation by declarant

Filing Requirements: None

Other: Provision for designation of a proxy to make health care decisions on behalf of declarant

ILLINOIS

Title of state's Living Will law: "Living Will Act"
Department of Public Health: (217) 782-4977
Minimum age to have a Living Will: 18 or emancipated minor
Witness Requirements: Two, 18 or older
Revocation Requirements:
- Physical destruction or defacement, or
- Written revocation, signed and dated, or
- Oral revocation in presence of witness 18 or older who signs and dates a writing confirming the revocation

Filing Requirements: Declarant must notify attending physician of existence of declaration, to be included in medical records

Other: None

INDIANA

Title of state's Living Will law: "Living Wills and Life-Prolonging Procedures Act"
State Board of Health: (317) 633-8400
Minimum age to have a Living Will: 18
Witness Requirements:
- Two, over 18
- Cannot sign Living Will on behalf of declarant
- No parent, spouse, or child
- No potential claim to declarant's estate
- Not directly financially responsible for declarant's medical care

Revocation Requirements:
- Physical destruction or defacement, or
- Written revocation, signed and dated, or
- Oral revocation

Filing Requirements: Declarant must notify attending physician for filing directive with medical records

Other: None

IOWA

Title of state's Living Will law: "Life Sustaining Procedures Act"

Department of Health: (515) 281-5605

Minimum age to have a Living Will: 18

Witness Requirements: Two

Revocation Requirements: By any manner declarant can communicate intent to revoke

Filing Requirements: Declarant must provide notification to attending physician

Other: None

KANSAS

Title of state's Living Will law: "Natural Death Act"

Department of Health and Environment: (913) 296-1343

Minimun age to have a Living Will: 18

Witness Requirements:
- Two or more, over 18
- Not the person who signed declaration on behalf of declarant
- Not related by blood or marriage
- Not entitled to estate of declarant by will or operation of law
- Not directly financially responsible for declarant's medical care

Revocation Requirements:
- Physical destruction or defacement, or
- Written revocation, signed and dated, or
- Oral revocation, in presence of witness, 18 or older, who signs and dates a written confirmation

Filing Requirements: Declarant must notify attending physician for filing with medical records

Other: None

KENTUCKY

Title of state's Living Will law: "Kentucky Living Will Act"

Department of Health: (502) 564-3970

Minimum age to have a Living Will: 18

Witness Requirements:
- Two, over 18 years, unrelated by blood, marriage
- No beneficiary of declarant under intestate laws
- Not the attending physician of declarant or employee of health care facility in which declarant is a patient
- Not directly financially responsible for declarant's health care

Revocation Requirements:
- Oral statement by declarant of intent to revoke, or
- Written revocation, signed and dated by declarant, or
- Physical destruction or defacement

Filing Requirements: Declarant must notify attending physician of execution of declaration

Other: None

LOUISIANA

Title of state's Living Will law: "Natural Death Act"

Department of Health and Hospitals: (504) 568-5050

Minimum age to have a Living Will: 18

Witness Requirements:
- Two competent adults, not related to declarant by blood or marriage
- Not entitled to any portion of estate of declarant upon decease

Revocation Requirements:
- Physical destruction or defacement, or
- Written revocation, signed and dated by declarant, or
- Oral or nonverbal revocation

Filing Requirements: Declarant must notify attending physician for filing in medical records

Other:
- Provision for oral or nonverbal declaration in presence of two witnesses at any time subsequent to the diagnosis of a terminal and irreversible condition
- Provision for comatose or incompetent patients who are diagnosed as having a terminal and irreversible condition and have not executed a declaration to have a declaration executed on their behalf by certain individuals

MAINE

Title of state's Living Will law: "Living Will Act"

Department of Human Services: (207) 289-2736

Minimum age to have a Living Will: 18

Witness Requirements: Two (no other requirements)
Revocation Requirements: In any manner, if communicated to attending physician or health care provider by declarant or one who witnessed the revocation
Filing Requirements: Declarant must provide copy to attending physician for filing with medical records
Other: None

MARYLAND

Title of state's Living Will law: "Life Sustaining Procedures Act"
Department of Health and Mental Hygiene: (301) 225-6500
Minimum age to have a Living Will: 18
Witness Requirements:
- Two, over 18 years
- Unrelated by blood or marriage
- Not a creditor or knowingly entitled to any portion of the estate of declarant
- Not financially or otherwise responsible for declarant's medical care or an employee of such person or institution

Revocation Requirements:
- Written revocation, signed and dated by declarant or person acting at direction of declarant, or
- Physical destruction or defacement, or
- Oral revocation, after declarant learns of a terminal condition

Filing Requirements: Declarant must notify attending physician for filing with medical records
Other: None

MASSACHUSETTS

Title of state's Living Will law: [No law]
Department of Public Health: (617) 727-2700
Minimum age to have a Living Will: 18
Witness Requirements:
- Two, over 18, unrelated by blood, marriage, or adoption
- No potential claim to declarant's estate, by will or operation of law
- Not a physician or his/her employee, nor an employee or patient at health care facility in which declarant is a patient
- NOTE: **If declarant is a patient in a nursing home or boarding facility at time of execution, it is advisable to have the director of that facility, or any designated patient advocate, act as a third witness to the Living Will**

Revocation Requirements:
- Physical destruction or defacement, or
- Written revocation, signed and dated in presence of at least one witness, 18 or over, or
- Verbal revocation in presence of a witness 18 or over who signs and dates a written confirmation

Filing Requirements: Copy of executed Living Will should be given to attending physician for filing with declarant's medical records
Other: None

MICHIGAN

Title of state's Living Will law: [No law]
Department of Public Health: (517) 335-8024
Minimum age to have a Living Will: 18
Witness Requirements:
- Two, over 18, unrelated by blood, marriage, or adoption
- No potential claim to declarant's estate, by will or operation of law
- Not a physician or his/her employee, nor employee or patient at health care facility in which declarant is a patient
- NOTE: **If declarant is a patient in a nursing home or boarding facility at time of execution, it is advisable to have the director of that facility, or any designated patient advocate, act as a third witness to the Living Will**

Revocation Requirements:
- Physical destruction or defacement, or
- Written revocation, signed and dated in presence of at least one witness, 18 or over, or
- Verbal revocation in presence of witness 18 or over who signs and dates a written confirmation

Filing Requirements: Copy of executed Living Will should be given to attending physician for filing with declarant's medical records
Other: None

MINNESOTA

Title of state's Living Will law: "Adult Health Care Decisions Act"
Department of Health: (612) 623-5460
Minimum age to have a Living Will: 18
Witness Requirements:
- Two, *or* a notary public
- Neither witness nor notary may be named proxy
- Not entitled to any portion of declarant's estate, by will or operation of law

Revocation Requirements:
- By any manner if communicated to attending physician or other health care provider by declarant, or
- If declarant's marriage is dissolved or annulled after execution of a declaration, former spouse is precluded from acting as proxy to make health care decisions for declarant (see "Other" below)

Filing Requirements: Declarant must deliver to physician or other health care provider

Other: Provision for designation of a proxy to make health care decisions on behalf of declarant

MISSISSIPPI

Title of state's Living Will law: "Natural Death Act"
Department of Health: (601) 354-6646
Minimum age to have a Living Will: 18 and mentally competent
Witness Requirements:
- Two or more
- Not related by blood or marriage
- No potential claim to declarant's estate
- Not attending physician or employee
- Not an employee of health facility in which declarant is a patient

Revocation Requirements:
- Written revocation, signed and dated by declarant and at least two witnesses who are qualified in some manner as declaration witnesses; written revocation must be filed with Bureau of Vital Statistics of State Board of Health, or
- If physically unable to execute a written revocation, a clear expression, oral or otherwise, of intent to revoke is effective

Filing Requirements: Declaration must be filed with the Bureau of Vital Statistics of the State Board of Health

Other: None

MISSOURI

Title of state's Living Will law: "Life Support Declaration"
Department of Health: (314) 751-6001
Minimum age to have a Living Will: 18
Witness Requirements:
- Two or more, over 18
- Not the person who signed on behalf or at direction of declarant

Revocation Requirements: By any manner declarant is able to communicate intent to revoke
Filing Requirements: Declarant must notify attending physician for filing with medical records
Other: None

MONTANA

Title of state's Living Will law: "Living Will Act"
Health Services Division: (406) 444-2037
Minimum age to have a Living Will: 18
Witness Requirements: Two
Revocation Requirements: By any manner declarant is able to communicate intent to revoke
Filing Requirements: Declarant must notify physician for filing with medical records
Other: None

NEBRASKA

Title of state's Living Will law: No title
Department of Health: (402) 471-2133
Minimum age to have a Living Will: 18
Witness Requirements:
- Two, over 18, unrelated by blood, marriage, or adoption
- No potential claim to declarant's estate, by will or operation of law
- Not a physician or his/her employee, nor employee or patient at health care facility in which declarant is a patient
- NOTE: **If declarant is a patient in a nursing home or boarding facility at time of execution, it is advisable to have the director of that facility, or any designated patient advocate, act as a third witness to the Living Will**

Revocation Requirements:
- Physical destruction or defacement, or
- Written revocation, signed and dated in presence of at least one witness, 18 or over, or
- Verbal revocation in presence of witness 18 or over who signs and dates a written confirmation

Filing Requirements: Copy of executed Living Will should be given to attending physician for filing with declarant's medical records
Other: None

NEVADA

Title of state's Living Will law: No title
Department of Human Resources: (702) 885-4740

Minimum age to have a Living Will: 18
Witness Requirements:
- Two adults
- Not related by blood or marriage
- Not attending physician or his/her employee
- Not an employee of the medical facility in which declarant is a patient
- No claim against estate of declarant

Revocation Requirements:
- Written revocation, or
- Verbal expression, when communicated to attending physician by declarant or one directed by declarant

Filing Requirements: Declarant must notify attending physician for filing in medical records
Other: None

NEW HAMPSHIRE

Title of state's Living Will law: "Terminal Care Document"
Department of Health and Welfare: (603) 271-4505
Minimum age to have a Living Will: 18
Witness Requirements:
- Two or more
- Not a spouse or heir at law
- Not attending physician or person acting under the direction or control of attending physician
- No claim against estate of declarant

Revocation Requirements:
- Physical destruction or defacement, or
- Oral revocation in presence of two or more witnesses, none a spouse or heir at law (anybody inheriting any part of an estate when someone dies without a Last Will and Testament), or
- Written revocation, signed and dated in presence of two or more witnesses, none a spouse or heir at law

Filing Requirements: Declarant must request attending physician to file with medical records
Other: If declarant is a patient in hospital or skilled nursing facility, additional witness must be chief of hospital medical staff or medical director of skilled nursing facility

NEW JERSEY

Title of state's Living Will law: [No law]
Department of Health: (609) 275-8714
Minimum age to have a Living Will: 18

Witness Requirements:
- Two, over 18, unrelated by blood, marriage, or adoption
- No potential claim to declarant's estate, by will or operation of law
- Not a physician or his/her employee, nor employee or patient at health care facility in which declarant is a patient
- **NOTE: If declarant is a patient in a nursing home or boarding facility at time of execution, it is advisable to have the director of that facility, or any designated patient advocate, act as a third witness to the Living Will**

Revocation Requirements:
- Physical destruction or defacement, or
- Written revocation, signed and dated in presence of at least one witness, 18 or over, or
- Verbal revocation in presence of witness 18 or over who signs and dates a written confirmation

Filing Requirements: Copy of executed Living Will should be given to attending physician for filing with declarant's medical records
Other: None

NEW MEXICO

Title of state's Living Will law: "Right to Die Act"
Department of Health and Environment: (505) 984-2000
Minimum age to have a Living Will: 18
Witness Requirements: Two or more
Revocation Requirements:
- Physical destruction, or
- Contrary indication expressed in presence of one adult witness

Filing Requirements: None
Other: Provision for execution of a directive for benefit of a terminally ill minor or a minor in an irreversible coma

NEW YORK

Title of state's Living Will law: No title
Department of Health: (518) 474-2011
Minimum age to have a Living Will: 18
Witness Requirements:
- *Prior to or during hospitalization, written decision:* two witnesses, 18 or older
- *During hospitalization, oral decision:* two witnesses, 18 or older, one a physician affiliated with hospital in which declarant is being treated

Revocation Requirements: Written or oral declaration of revocation to a physician or member of the nursing staff where declarant is being treated

Filing Requirements: Copy of executed Living Will should be given to attending physician for filing with declarant's medical records

Other: Provides for surrogate decision making on behalf of minors or adult patients without capacity

NORTH CAROLINA

Title of state's Living Will law: "Natural Death Act"

Division of Health Services: (919) 733-3446

Minimum age to have a Living Will: None specified

Witness Requirements:

- Two, not related within the third degree to declarant or declarant's spouse
- No potential claim to declarant's estate
- Not attending physician or physician's employee
- Not employee of health care facility, nursing home, or group-care home in which declarant resides

Revocation Requirements: By any manner declarant is able to communicate intent to revoke

Filing Requirements: None

Other: None

NORTH DAKOTA

Title of state's Living Will law: "Uniform Rights of Terminally Ill Act"

Department of Health: (701) 224-2372

Minimum age to have a Living Will: 18

Witness Requirements:

- Two, unrelated by blood or marriage
- No potential claim to declarant's estate
- Not directly financially responsible for declarant's medical care
- Not an attending physician
- If declarant is resident in a long-term care facility, one of two witnesses must be a regional long-term care ombudsman

Revocation Requirements:

- Written revocation, signed and dated, or
- Physical destruction or defacement by declarant or another at declarant's direction and in his/her presence, or
- Oral revocation

Filing Requirements: None

Other:

- **Re-execution Requirements: Instrument ex-**

ecuted prior to July 10, 1989 is valid for five years from July 10, 1989, unless declarant becomes incompetent within five years of execution and remains incompetent at the time of determination of terminal condition

OHIO

Title of state's Living Will law: [No law]

Department of Health: (614) 466-2253

Minimum age to have a Living Will: 18

Witness Requirements:

- Two, over 18, unrelated by blood, marriage, or adoption
- No potential claim to declarant's estate, by will or operation of law
- Not a physician or his/her employee nor employee or patient at health care facility in which declarant is a patient
- NOTE: **If declarant is a patient in a nursing home or boarding facility at time of execution, it is advisable to have the director of that facility, or any designated patient advocate, act as a third witness to the Living Will**

Revocation Requirements:

- Physical destruction or defacement, or
- Written revocation, signed and dated in presence of at least one witness, 18 or over, or
- Verbal revocation in presence of witness 18 or over who signs and dates a written confirmation

Filing Requirements: Copy of executed Living Will should be given to the attending physician for filing with declarant's medical records

Other: None

OKLAHOMA

Title of state's Living Will law: "Oklahoma Natural Death Act"

Department of Health: (405) 271-4200

Minimum age to have a Living Will: 21

Witness Requirements:

- Two, over 21
- Not related by blood or marriage
- No potential claim to estate of declarant
- Not financially responsible for medical care of declarant
- Not attending physician or his/her employee or an employee of health care facility in which declarant is a patient
- Not a patient in same health care facility

Revocation Requirements:
- Physical destruction or defacement, or
- Written revocation, signed and dated, *only effective when received by attending physician,* or
- Oral revocation in presence of witness over 21 who signs and dates a written confirmation

Filing Requirements: None

Other: None

OREGON

Title of state's Living Will law: "Directive to Physicians"

Health Division: (503) 229-5032

Minimum age to have a Living Will: 18

Witness Requirements:
- Two, unrelated by blood or marriage
- No potential claim to declarant's estate
- Not attending physician or employee of physician or health facility in which declarant is a patient
- If declarant is a patient in a long-term care facility, one witness must be designated by the Department of Human Resources

Revocation Requirements:
- Physical destruction or defacement, or
- Written revocation, signed and dated, or
- Verbal revocation

Filing Requirements: Attending physician required to file directive with declarant's medical records

Other: None

PENNSYLVANIA

Title of state's Living Will law: [No law]

Department of Health: (717) 783-2500

Minimum age to have a Living Will: 18

Witness Requirements:
- Two, over 18, unrelated by blood, marriage, or adoption
- No potential claim to declarant's estate, by will or operation of law
- Not a physician or his/her employee, nor employee or patient at health care facility in which declarant is a patient
- **NOTE: If declarant is a patient in a nursing home or boarding facility at time of execution, it is advisable to have the director of that facility, or any designated patient advocate, act as a third witness to the Living Will**

Revocation Requirements:
- Physical destruction or defacement, or

- Written revocation, signed and dated in presence of at least one witness, 18 or over, or
- Verbal revocation in presence of witness 18 or over who signs and dates a written confirmation

Filing Requirements: Copy of executed Living Will should be given to the attending physician for filing with declarant's medical records

Other: None

RHODE ISLAND

Title of state's Living Will law: [No law]

Department of Health: (401) 277-2231

Minimum age to have a Living Will: 18

Witness Requirements:
- Two, over 18, unrelated by blood, marriage, or adoption
- No potential claim to declarant's estate, by will or operation of law
- Not a physician or his/her employee, nor employee or patient at health care facility in which declarant is a patient
- **NOTE: If declarant is a patient in a nursing home or boarding facility at time of execution, it is advisable to have the director of that facility, or any designated patient advocate, act as a third witness to the Living Will**

Revocation Requirements:
- Physical destruction or defacement, or
- Written revocation, signed and dated in presence of at least one witness, 18 or over, or
- Verbal revocation in presence of witness 18 or over who signs and dates a written confirmation

Filing Requirements: Copy of executed Living Will should be given to the attending physician for filing with declarant's medical records

Other: None

SOUTH CAROLINA

Title of state's Living Will law: "Death With Dignity Act"

Health and Environmental Control: (803) 734-4880

Minimum age to have a Living Will: 18

Witness Requirements:
- Two, not related by blood or marriage, either as spouse, lineal ancestor, descendant of parents of declarant, or spouse of any of them
- Not directly financially responsible for declarant's medical care

- Not entitled to any portion of the estate of declarant, not beneficiary of any life insurance policy of declarant
- No more than one witness is employee of health facility in which declarant is a patient
- Not attending physician or his/her employee
- **NOTE: If declarant is patient in a hospital or skilled or intermediate care nursing facility at time declaration is executed, one witness must be an ombudsman as designated by the State Ombudsman, Office of the Governor**

Revocation Requirements:
- Physical destruction or defacement, or
- Written revocation, signed and dated, if communicated to attending physician, or
- Oral revocation, communicated to attending physician

Filing Requirements: None

Other: All patients with life-threatening conditions diagnosed as terminal must be administered active treatment for at least six hours before physician may give effect to a declaration

SOUTH DAKOTA

Title of state's Living Will law: [No law]
Department of Health: (605) 773-3361
Minimum age to have a Living Will: 18
Witness Requirements:
- Two, over 18, unrelated by blood, marriage, or adoption
- No potential claim to declarant's estate, by will or operation of law
- Not a physician or his/her employee, nor employee or patient at health care facility in which declarant is a patient
- **NOTE: If declarant is a patient in a nursing home or boarding facility at time of execution, it is advisable to have the director of that facility, or any designated patient advocate, act as a third witness to the Living Will**

Revocation Requirements:
- Physical destruction or defacement, or
- Written revocation, signed and dated in presence of at least one witness, 18 or over, or
- Verbal revocation in presence of witness 18 or over who signs and dates a written confirmation

Filing Requirements: Copy of executed Living Will should be given to the attending physician for filing with declarant's medical records
Other: None

TENNESSEE

Title of state's Living Will law: "Tennessee Right to Natural Death Act"
Department of Health and Environment: (615) 741-3111
Minimum age to have a Living Will: 18
Witness Requirements:
- Two, unrelated by blood or marriage
- No potential claim to declarant's estate, by will or operation of law
- Not attending physician or his/her employee
- Not employee of health care facility in which declarant is a patient

Revocation Requirements:
- Written, signed, and dated by declarant and at least one witness, or notarized, or
- Orally, by declarant to attending physician

Filing Requirements: Declarant must provide copy to attending physician or health care provider to be filed with medical records
Other: None

TEXAS

Title of state's Living Will law: "Natural Death Act"
Department of Health: (512) 458-7375
Minimum age to have a Living Will: 18
Witness Requirements:
- Two, unrelated by blood or marriage
- No potential claim to declarant's estate
- Not attending physician or physician's employee
- No employee or patient in a health care facility in which declarant is a patient

Revocation Requirements:
- Physical destruction or defacement, or
- Written revocation, signed and dated, or
- Oral revocation

Filing Requirements: Declarant must notify attending physician to include directive in medical records
Other:
- Provision for nonwritten directive in presence of attending physician and two qualified witnesses
- Provision for directive on behalf of a minor

UTAH

Title of state's Living Will law: "Personal Choice and Living Will Act"
Department of Health: (801) 538-6111
Minimum age to have a Living Will: 18

Witness Requirements:
- Two or more, over 18
- Not related by blood or marriage
- No potential claim to declarant's estate
- Not directly financially responsible for declarant's medical care
- Not an agent of any health care facility in which declarant is a patient

Revocation Requirements:
- Physical destruction or defacement, or
- Written revocation, signed and dated, or
- Oral revocation, in presence of witness 18 or over who signs and dates a written confirmation

Filing Requirements: None
Other: Provision for special Power of Attorney

VERMONT

Title of state's Living Will law: "Terminal Care Document"
Department of Health: (802) 863-7280
Minimum age to have a Living Will: 18
Witness Requirements:
- Two or more
- Not spouse
- No potential claim to declarant's estate, by will or operation of law
- Not attending physician or acting under control or direction of attending physician

Revocation Requirements:
- Physical destruction or defacement by declarant or another at his/her direction and in his/her presence, or
- Orally, in presence of two or more witnesses, at least one not a spouse or relative

Filing Requirements: None
Other: None

VIRGINIA

Title of state's Living Will law: "Natural Death Act of Virginia"
Department of Health: (804) 786-3561
Minimum age to have a Living Will: 18
Witness Requirements: Two, not spouse or blood relative
Revocation Requirements:
- Written revocation, signed and dated, or
- Physical cancellation or destruction, or
- Oral revocation, if communicated to attending physician

Filing Requirements: Declarant must notify physi-

cian and original or copy filed with medical records
Other: Oral declaration may be made in the presence of a physician and two witnesses by any nonwritten means of communication at any time subsequent to diagnosis of a terminal condition

WASHINGTON

Title of state's Living Will law: "Natural Death Act"
Department of Health: (206) 586-5846
Minimum age to have a Living Will: 18
Witness Requirements:
- Two, unrelated by blood or marriage
- No potential claim to declarant's estate
- Not attending physician
- Not employee of attending physician or health facility in which declarant is a patient

Revocation Requirements:
- Physical destruction or defacement, or
- Written revocation, signed and dated, or
- Verbal revocation

Filing Requirements: Declarant must provide a copy to attending physician for filing with medical records
Other: None

WEST VIRGINIA

Title of state's Living Will law: "Natural Death Act"
Health and Human Resources Department: (304) 348-2400
Minimum age to have a Living Will: 18
Witness Requirements:
- Two or more, over 18
- Not related by marriage or blood
- Not signer of declaration on behalf of declarant
- Not knowingly having a potential claim to declarant's estate
- Not directly financially responsible for declarant's medical care
- Not attending physician or his/her employee or employee of health facility in which declarant is a patient

Revocation Requirements:
- Physical destruction, or
- Written revocation, signed and dated by declarant or person acting at direction of declarant, or
- Verbal revocation in presence of witness, 18 or older, who signs and dates a written confirmation

Filing Requirements: Declarant must notify attending physician who shall make original or copy part of medical records
Other: None

WISCONSIN

Title of state's Living Will law: "Natural Death Act"
Health and Social Services Department: (608) 266-1511
Minimum age to have a Living Will: 18
Witness Requirements:
- Two, not related by blood or marriage
- No potential claim to declarant's estate
- Not attending physician, attending nurse, or attending medical staff
- Not an employee of attending physician
- Not an employee of inpatient health care facility in which declarant is a patient, if the employee is involved in medical care of declarant

Revocation Requirements:
- Physical destruction or defacement, or
- Written revocation, signed and dated, or
- Verbal revocation

Filing Requirements: Declarant must notify attending physician of existence of declaration, and physician must make original declaration part of medical records
Other: None

WYOMING

Title of state's Living Will law: "Living Will"
Health and Social Services Department: (307) 777-7121
Minimum age to have a Living Will: 18
Witness Requirements:
- Two or more
- Not related by blood or marriage
- Not signer of declaration on behalf of declarant
- No potential claim to declarant's estate
- Not directly financially responsible for declarant's medical care

Revocation Requirements:
- Physical destruction or defacement, or
- Written revocation, signed and dated by declarant or person acting at direction of declarant, or
- Verbal revocation, in presence of adult witness who signs and dates a writing confirming the revocation

Filing Requirements: Declarant must provide a copy to attending physician to file with medical records
Other: Provision for designation of a proxy to make health care decisions on behalf of declarant

LIVING WILL FORMS

INSTRUCTIONS

IMPORTANT: Read all instructions before beginning to fill out your Living Will form.

Do not sign your name unless your witnesses and a notary are present.

Check the box as you complete each instruction:

☐ 1. Select the form for your state. We recommend that you carefully cut it out of the book.

☐ 2. Review your state's entry in the state-by-state guide (Chapter 8), **especially for the witnessing requirements.**

☐ 3. Read over the Living Will form for your state. If you find anything in the form confusing, refer to:
- the state-by-state guide (Chapter 8), or
- the Glossary at the end of this book (page 97), or
- the question-and-answer portion of this book (Chapters 3 through 7)
- review the Checklist of Medical Interventions (page 33); if necessary, discuss it with your physician

☐ 4. Identify two witnesses who meet your state's requirements (again, refer to the state-by-state guide, Chapter 8).

☐ 5. In the presence of your witnesses, fill in your form.

☐ 6. When entering your name, be certain to print or type it as you commonly use it. Do not use a nickname, but enter your name as you use it on your bank account or tax return.

☐ 7. If you make a mistake or want to change your form, wait until your witnesses and a notary are present before altering it.

☐ 8. In the presence of, and with the guidance of, a notary, sign your Living Will form. Then have your witnesses sign it.

☐ 9. Make copies of your executed Living Will form and the Checklist of Medical Interventions and distribute them to your physician, and to others as you wish.

☐ 10. Be sure to consult the state-by-state guide (Chapter 8) and fulfill any filing requirements that your state's Living Will law might require.

☐ 11. Turn to your Living Will record (page 35). Carefully cut it out, complete the appropriate sections, and file and maintain it as suggested.

☐ 12. To re-execute your Living Will, simply resign and date your current Living Will.

CHECKLIST OF MEDICAL INTERVENTIONS

Although the Living Will forms in this book are taken directly from the applicable state statutes, many contain somewhat vague terms, such as "heroic" or "extraordinary" measures, or "life sustaining" procedures. To ensure that your wishes are expressed as clearly as possible, it is strongly suggested that you discuss the following checklist with your physician to determine what medical interventions meet with your approval. Then have your physician keep a list of those medical interventions that you choose in your medical file with a copy of your Living Will. Your physician can explain in *detail* the procedures *outlined* here, so that your choice is truly an informed one.

CHECKLIST OF MEDICAL INTERVENTIONS
(To Be Discussed with Your Physician)

☐ **pain medication:** narcotics and other drugs administered to reduce pain

☐ **antibiotic treatment:** the use of drugs to fight bacterial infection

☐ **blood transfusion**

☐ **simple diagnostic test:** blood test, X ray, et cetera

☐ **invasive diagnostic test:** a more complex test that may require cutting of the skin or the insertion of an instrument (cardiac catheterization, et cetera)

☐ **chemotherapy:** treatment of cancer with drugs, which may have substantial side effects

☐ **kidney dialysis:** mechanical removal of waste from blood

☐ **minor surgery:** a minor operative procedure

☐ **major surgery:** a more difficult and potentially dangerous procedure

☐ **organ transplantation:** replacement of a diseased organ with the organ of another person

☐ **mechanically-assisted breathing:** may require the insertion of a tube into the windpipe

☐ **cardiopulmonary resuscitation (CPR):** techniques for stimulating a stopped heart

☐ **artificial nutrition and hydration:**
  • intravenous feeding
  • nasogastric intubation (nourishment through a tube from the nose to the stomach)
  • gastrostomy (nourishment through a tube surgically implanted in the stomach)

NOTES

YOUR LIVING WILL RECORD

It is strongly recommended that you maintain and keep this record of your Living Will somewhere handy and safe—perhaps with your calendar, an address book, or your current tax returns—so that both you and your family can easily find it.

- Date of execution (the date your Living Will was notarized): _____
- Names and Addresses of Witnesses:

_____ _____

_____ _____

_____ _____

- Location of your original (notarized) Living Will: _____
- Copies given to:

_____ _____

_____ _____

_____ _____

_____ _____

- Your Living Will review and re-execution:

  ☐ Two-year review: _____
  (date)

  ☐ Four-year review: _____
  (date)

  ☐ Five-year re-execution: _____
  (date)

LIVING WILL DECLARATION

To my family, relatives, friends, physicians, clergy, and all others whom it may concern:

Declaration made this _____ day of _____, 19 _____ (month, year).

I, _____ (full name), being of sound mind, willfully, and voluntarily make known my desires that my life shall not be artificially prolonged under the circumstances set forth below, do declare:

1) If at any time I should have an incurable injury, disease, illness, or condition certified to be terminal by two physicians who have personally examined me, one of whom is my attending physician, and the physicians have determined that my death is imminent, whether or not life-sustaining procedures are utilized and where the application of life-sustaining procedures would serve only to artificially prolong the dying process; or alternatively, if I have been diagnosed as being in a persistent vegetative state, I direct that all artificial life-sustaining procedures be withheld or withdrawn and that I be permitted to die naturally with only the administration of nutrition, medication, or the performance of any medical procedure deemed necessary to provide me with comfort care or to alleviate pain.

2) In the absence of my ability to give further directions regarding my treatment, including life-sustaining procedures, it is my intention that this declaration be honored by my family and physicians as the final expression of my legal right to refuse or accept medical and surgical treatment, and I accept the consequences of such refusal.

3) I understand the full importance of this declaration and am emotionally and mentally competent to make this declaration. No participant in the making of this declaration or in its being carried into effect, whether it be a physician, spouse, relative, or any other person shall be held responsible in any way, legally, professionally, or socially, for complying with my directions.

_____
Declarant's signature

The declarant is personally known to me and is, to my judgment, of sound mind.
I am at least 18 years of age and
- not related to declarant by blood, marriage, or adoption
- not the declarant's attending physician or employee of the attending physician, or a patient or employee of the medical care facility in which declarant is a patient
- not entitled to any portion of the declarant's estate on declarant's death
- have no claim against any portion of the declarant's estate on declarant's death

Witness _____

Address _____

Witness _____

Address _____

County of _____

State of _____

Subscribed, sworn to and acknowledged before me by _____, the declarant, and

subscribed and sworn to before me by _____ and _____, witnesses,

this _____ day of _____, 19 _____.

My commission expires:

_____
Notary Public

[Seal]

Form #1

DECLARATION

Declaration made this _____ day of _____ (month, year).

I, _____, being of sound mind, willfully and voluntarily make known my desires that my dying shall not be artificially prolonged under the circumstances set forth below, do declare:

If at any time I should have an incurable injury, disease or illness certified to be a terminal condition by two physicians who have personally examined me, one of whom is my attending physician, and the physicians have determined that my death will occur whether or not life-sustaining procedures are utilized and where the application of life-sustaining procedures would serve only to artificially prolong the dying process, I direct that such procedures be withheld or withdrawn, and that I be permitted to die naturally with only the administration of nutrition, medication or the performance of any medical procedure deemed necessary to provide me with comfort care or to alleviate pain.

In the absence of my ability to give directions regarding the use of such life-sustaining procedures, it is my intention that this declaration be honored by my family and physician(s) as the final expression of my legal right to refuse medical or surgical treatment and accept the consequences resulting from such refusal.

I understand the full import of this declaration and I am emotionally and mentally competent to make this declaration.

Signed _____

Address _____

_____

I did not sign the declarant's signature above for or at the direction of the declarant. I am at least eighteen years of age and am not related to the declarant by blood or marriage, entitled to any portion of the estate of the declarant according to the laws of intestate succession of the State of _____ or to the best of my knowledge under any will of declarant or codicil thereto, or directly financially responsible for declarant's medical care. I am not the declarant's attending physician, an employee of the attending physician, nor an employee of the health facility in which the declarant is a patient.

Witness _____

Witness _____

STATE OF _____ ,

COUNTY OF _____ , to-wit:

This day personally appeared before me, the undersigned authority, a Notary Public in and for _____

County, _____ (State), _____ (witness) and

_____ (witness) who, being first duly sworn, say that they are the subscribing

witnesses to the declaration of _____ (declarant), which declaration is dated the

_____ day of _____, 19 _____; and that on the said date the said _____ (declarant), the declarant, signed, sealed, published and declared the same as and for his declaration, in the presence of both these affiants; and that these affiants, at the request of said declarant, in the presence of each other, and in the presence of said declarant, all present at the same time, signed their names as attesting witnesses to said declaration.

Affiants further say that this affidavit is made at the request of _____ (declarant),

declarant, and in his presence, and that _____ (declarant), at the time the declaration was executed, was in the opinion of affiants, of sound mind and memory, and over the age of eighteen years.

_____

_____

Taken, subscribed and sworn to before me by _____ (witness) and

_____ (witness) this _____ day of _____, 19 _____.

My commission expires:

_____
Notary Public

Form #2

LIVING WILL

I, _____, willfully and voluntarily make known my desire that my dying shall not be artificially prolonged under the circumstances set forth below, and do hereby declare:

If at any time I should have a terminal condition and my attending physician has determined that there can be no recovery from such condition and my death is imminent, where the application of life-prolonging procedures would serve only to artificially prolong the dying process. I direct that such procedures be withheld or withdrawn, and that I be permitted to die naturally with only the administration of medications or the performance of any medical procedure deemed necessary to provide me with comfortable care or to alleviate pain. In the absence of my ability to give directions regarding the use of such life-prolonging procedures, it is my intention that this declaration shall be honored by my family and physician as the final expression of my legal right to refuse medical or surgical treatment and accept the consequences of such refusal. I understand the full import of this declaration, and I am emotionally and mentally competent to make this declaration. In acknowledgment whereof, I do hereinafter affix my signature on this the _____ day of

_____, 19_____.

_____
Declarant

We, the subscribing witnesses hereto, are personally acquainted with and subscribe our names hereto at the request of the declarant, an adult, whom we believe to be of sound mind, fully aware of the action taken herein and its possible consequence.

We, the undersigned witnesses, further declare that we are not related to the declarant by blood or marriage; that we are not entitled to any portion of the estate of the declarant upon his decease under any will or codicil thereto presently existing or by operation of law then existing; that we are not the attending physician, an employee of the attending physician or a health facility in which the declarant is a patient; and that we are not a person who, at the present time, has a claim against any portion of the estate of the declarant upon his death.

_____
Witness

_____
Witness

County of _____

State of _____

Subscribed, sworn to and acknowledged before me by _____,

the declarant, and subscribed and sworn to before me by _____

and _____, witnesses, this _____ day of _____, 19_____.

_____
Notary Public

Form #3

DIRECTIVE TO PHYSICIANS

Directive made this _____ day of _____ (month, year).

I _____, being of sound mind, willfully and voluntarily make known my desire that my life shall not be artificially prolonged under the circumstances set forth in this directive.

   1. If at any time I should have an incurable condition caused by injury, disease, or illness certified to be a terminal condition by two physicians, and if the application of life-sustaining procedures would serve only to artificially postpone the moment of my death, and if my attending physician determines that my death is imminent whether or not life-sustaining procedures are used, I direct that those procedures be withheld or withdrawn, and that I be permitted to die naturally.

   2. In the absence of my ability to give directions regarding the use of those life-sustaining procedures, it is my intention that this directive be honored by my family and physicians as the final expression of my legal right to refuse medical or surgical treatment and accept the consequences from that refusal.

   3. If I have been diagnosed as pregnant and that diagnosis is known to my physician, this directive has no effect during my pregnancy.

   4. This directive is in effect until it is revoked.

   5. I understand the full import of this directive and I am emotionally and mentally competent to make this directive.

   6. I understand that I may revoke this directive at any time.

Signed _____

(City, County, and State of Residence)

The declarant has been personally known to me and I believe the declarant to be of sound mind. I am not related to the declarant by blood or marriage. I would not be entitled to any portion of the declarant's estate on the declarant's death. I am not the attending physician of the declarant or an employee of the attending physician or a health facility in which the declarant is a patient. I am not a patient in the health care facility in which the declarant is a patient. I have no claim against any portion of the declarant's estate on the declarant's death.

Witness _____

Witness _____

County of _____

State of _____

Before me, the undersigned authority, personally appeared _____,

_____, and _____ known to me to be Declarant and the Witnesses whose names are signed to the foregoing instrument, and who, in the presence of each other, did subscribe their names to the Declaration on this date.

My commission expires:

_____

Notary Public

[Seal]

Form #4

DECLARATION

If I should have an incurable or irreversible condition that will cause my death within a relatively short time, it is my desire that my life not be prolonged by administration of life-sustaining procedures.

If my condition is terminal and I am unable to participate in decisions regarding my medical treatment, I direct my attending physician to withhold or withdraw procedures that merely prolong the dying process and are not necessary to my comfort or to alleviate pain.

I [ ] do [ ] do not desire that nutrition or hydration (food and water) be provided by gastric tube or intravenously if necessary.

Signed this _____ day of _____, _____.

Signature _____

Place _____

The declarant is known to me and voluntarily signed or voluntarily directed another to sign this document in my presence.

Witness _____

Address _____

Witness _____

Address _____

State of _____

_____ Judicial District

The foregoing instrument was acknowledged before me this _____ by _____.
                                                          (date)   (name of person who acknowledged)

_____
Signature of Person Taking Acknowledgment

_____
Title or Rank

_____
Serial Number, if any

Form #5

DECLARATION

If I should have an incurable or irreversible condition that will cause my death within a relatively short time, and I am no longer able to make decisions regarding my medical treatment, I direct my attending physician, pursuant to the Arkansas Rights of the Terminally Ill or Permanently Unconscious Act, to withhold or withdraw treatment that only prolongs the process of dying and is not necessary to my comfort or to alleviate pain.

Signed this _____ day of _____, _____

Signature _____

Address _____

The declarant voluntarily signed this writing in my presence.

Witness _____

Address _____

Witness _____

Address _____

County of _____

State of _____

Before me, the undersigned authority, personally appeared _____,

_____, and _____

known to me to be Declarant and the Witnesses whose names are signed to the foregoing instrument, and who, in the presence of each other, did subscribe their names to the Declaration on this date.

My commission expires:

_____

Notary Public

[Seal]

Form #6

DIRECTIVE TO PHYSICIANS

Directive made this _____ day of _____ (month, year).

I _____, being of sound mind, willfully, and voluntarily make known my desire that my life shall not be artificially prolonged under the circumstances set forth below, do hereby declare:

1. If at any time I should have an incurable injury, disease, or illness certified to be a terminal condition by two physicians, and where the application of life-sustaining procedures would serve only to artificially prolong the moment of my death and where my physician determines that my death is imminent whether or not life-sustaining procedures are utilized, I direct that such procedures be withheld or withdrawn, and that I be permitted to die naturally.

2. In the absence of my ability to give directions regarding the use of such life-sustaining procedures, it is my intention that this directive shall be honored by my family and physician(s) as the final expression of my legal right to refuse medical or surgical treatment and accept the consequences from such refusal.

3. If I have been diagnosed as pregnant and that diagnosis is known to my physician, this directive shall have no force or effect during the course of my pregnancy.

4. I have been diagnosed and notified at least 14 days ago as having a terminal condition by _____, M.D., whose address is _____, and whose telephone number is _____. I understand that if I have not filled in the physician's name and address, it shall be presumed that I did not have a terminal condition when I made out this directive.

5. This directive shall have no force or effect five years from the date filled in above.

6. I understand the full import of this directive and I am emotionally and mentally competent to make this directive.

Signed _____

City, County and State of Residence _____

The declarant has been personally known to me and I believe him or her to be of sound mind.

Witness _____

Witness _____

County of _____

State of _____

Before me, the undersigned authority, personally appeared _____, _____, and _____ known to me to be Declarant and the Witnesses whose names are signed to the foregoing instrument, and who, in the presence of each other, did subscribe their names to the Declaration on this date.

My commission expires:

_____
Notary Public

[Seal]

Form #7

DECLARATION AS TO MEDICAL OR SURGICAL TREATMENT

I, _____ (name of declarant), being of sound mind and at least eighteen years of age, direct that my life shall not be artificially prolonged under the circumstances set forth below and hereby declare that:

1. If at any time my attending physician and one other physician certify in writing that:

a. I have an injury, disease, or illness which is not curable or reversible and which, in their judgment, is a terminal condition: and

b. For a period of forty-eight consecutive hours or more, I have been unconscious, comatose, or otherwise incompetent so as to be unable to make or communicate responsible decisions concerning my person: then

I direct that life-sustaining procedures shall be withdrawn and withheld, it being understood that life-sustaining procedures shall not include any medical procedure or intervention for nourishment or considered necessary by the attending physician to provide comfort or alleviate pain.

2. I execute this declaration, as my free and voluntary act, this _____ day of _____ , 19_____ .

By _____

Declarant

The foregoing instrument was signed and declared by _____ to be his declaration, in the presence of us, who, in his presence, in the presence of each other, and at his request, have signed our names below as witnesses, and we declare that, at the time of the execution of this instrument, the declarant, according to our best knowledge and belief, was of sound mind and under no constraint or undue influence.

Dated at _____ , Colorado, this _____ day of _____ , 19 _____ .

_____

Name and Address

_____

Name and Address

STATE OF _____)

) ss.

County of _____)

SUBSCRIBED and sworn to before me by _____ ,

the declarant, and _____ , and _____ , witnesses, as the voluntary act and deed of the declarant, this _____ day of _____ , 19 _____ .

My commission expires:

_____

Notary Public

Form #8

DECLARATION

If the time comes when I am incapacitated to the point when I can no longer actively take part in decisions for my own life, and am unable to direct my physician as to my own medical care, I wish this statement to stand as a testament of my wishes. I _____ (name) request that I be allowed to die and not be kept alive through life support systems if my condition is deemed terminal. I do not intend any direct taking of my life, but only that my dying not be unreasonably prolonged. This request is made, after careful reflection, while I am of sound mind.

_____ (Signature)

_____ (Date)

_____ (Witness)

_____ (Witness)

County of _____

State of _____

Before me, the undersigned authority, personally appeared _____,

_____, and _____

known to me to be Declarant and the Witnesses whose names are signed to the foregoing instrument, and who, in the presence of each other, did subscribe their names to the Declaration on this date.

My commission expires:

_____

Notary Public

[Seal]

DECLARATION

Declaration made this _____ day of _____, 19 _____.

I, _____, willfully and voluntarily make known my desire that my dying not be artificially prolonged under the circumstances set forth below, and I do hereby declare:

If at any time I should have a terminal condition and if my attending physician has determined that there can be no recovery from such condition and that my death is imminent, I direct that life-prolonging procedures be withheld or withdrawn when the application of such procedures would serve only to prolong artificially the process of dying, and that I be permitted to die naturally with only the administration of medication or the performance of any medical procedure deemed necessary to provide me with comfort care or to alleviate pain. I do ( ) I do not ( ) desire that nutrition and hydration (food and water) be withheld or withdrawn when the application of such procedures would serve only to prolong artificially the process of dying.

In the absence of my ability to give directions regarding the use of such life-prolonging procedures, it is my intention that this declaration be honored by my family and physician as the final expression of my legal right to refuse medical or surgical treatment and to accept the consequences for such refusal.

If I have been diagnosed as pregnant and that diagnosis is known to my physician, this declaration shall have no force or effect during the course of my pregnancy.

I understand the full import of this declaration, and I am emotionally and mentally competent to make this declaration.

_____
(Signed)

The declarant is known to me, and I believe him or her to be of sound mind.

_____
Witness

_____
Witness

County of _____

State of _____

Before me, the undersigned authority, personally appeared _____,

_____, and _____

known to me to be Declarant and the Witnesses whose names are signed to the foregoing instrument, and who, in the presence of each other, did subscribe their names to the Declaration on this date.

My commission expires:

_____
Notary Public

[Seal]

Form #10

LIVING WILL

Living will made this _____ day of _____ (month, year).

I, _____, being of sound mind, willfully and voluntarily make known my desire that my life shall not be prolonged under the circumstances set forth below and do declare:

1. If at any time I should have a terminal condition as defined in and established in accordance with the procedures set forth in paragraph (10) of Code Section 31-32-2 of the Official Code of Georgia Annotated, I direct that the application of life-sustaining procedures to my body be withheld or withdrawn and that I be permitted to die;

2. In the absence of my ability to give directions regarding the use of such life-sustaining procedures, it is my intention that this living will shall be honored by my family and physician(s) as the final expression of my legal right to refuse medical or surgical treatment and accept the consequences from such refusal;

3. This will shall have no force or effect seven years from the date I signed this document as stated above; however, I understand that, if at the end of said seven years I am incapable of communicating with the attending physician, this will shall remain in effect until such time as I am able to communicate with the physician;

4. I understand that I may revoke this living will at any time;

5. I understand the full import of this living will, and I am at least 18 years of age and am emotionally and mentally competent to make this living will; and

6. If I have been diagnosed as pregnant, this living will shall have no force and effect during the course of my pregnancy.

Signed _____

_____ (City), _____ (County), and

_____ (State of Residence).

I hereby witness this living will and attest that:

(1) The declarant is personally known to me and I believe the declarant to be at least 18 years of age and of sound mind;

(2) I am at least 18 years of age;

(3) To the best of my knowledge, at the time of the execution of this living will, I:

(A) Am not related to the declarant by blood or marriage;

(B) Would not be entitled to any portion of the declarant's estate by any will or by operation of law under the rules of descent and distribution of this state;

(C) Am not the attending physician of declarant or an employee of the attending physician or an employee of the hospital or skilled nursing facility in which declarant is a patient;

(D) Am not directly financially responsible for the declarant's medical care; and

(E) Have no present claim against any portion of the estate of the declarant;

(4) Declarant has signed this document in my presence as above-instructed, on the date above first shown.

Witness _____

Address _____

Witness _____

Address _____

Additional witness required when living will is signed in a hospital or skilled nursing facility.

I hereby witness this living will and attest that I believe the declarant to be of sound mind and to have made this living will willingly and voluntarily.

Witness: _____

Medical director of skilled nursing facility or chief of the hospital medical staff

County of _____

State of _____

Form #11

Before me, the undersigned authority, personally appeared _____,

_____, _____,

and _____ known to me to be Declarant and the Witnesses whose names are signed to the foregoing instrument, and who, in the presence of each other, did subscribe their names to the Declaration on this date.

My commission expires:

_____
                                            Notary Public

[Seal]

A LIVING WILL

A Directive to Withhold or to Provide Treatment

To my family, my relatives, my friends, my physicians, my employers, and all others whom it may concern:

Directive made this _____ day of _____ 19_____

I, _____ (name), being of sound mind, willfully, and voluntarily make known my desire that my life shall not be prolonged artificially under the circumstances set forth below, do hereby declare:

1. If at any time I should have an incurable injury, disease, illness or condition certified to be terminal by two medical doctors who have examined me, and where the application of life-sustaining procedures of any kind would serve only to prolong artificially the moment of my death, and where a medical doctor determines that my death is imminent, whether or not life-sustaining procedures are utilized, or I have been diagnosed as being in a persistent vegetative state, I direct that the following marked expression of my intent be followed and that I be permitted to die naturally, and that I receive any medical treatment or care that may be required to keep me free of pain or distress.

Check One Box:

☐ If at any time I should become unable to communicate my instructions, then I direct that all medical treatment, care, and nutrition and hydration necessary to restore my health, sustain my life, and to abolish or alleviate pain or distress be provided to me. Nutrition and hydration shall not be withheld or withdrawn from me if I would die from malnutrition or dehydration rather than from my injury, disease, illness or condition.

☐ If at any time I should become unable to communicate my instructions and where the application of artificial life-sustaining procedures shall serve only to prolong artificially the moment of my death, I direct such procedures be withheld or withdrawn except for the administration of nutrition and hydration.

☐ If at any time I should become unable to communicate my instructions and where the application of artificial life-sustaining procedures shall serve only to prolong artificially the moment of death, I direct such procedures be withheld or withdrawn including withdrawal of the administration of nutrition and hydration.

2. In the absence of my ability to give directions regarding the use of life-sustaining procedures, I hereby appoint

_____ (name) currently residing at _____, as my attorney-in-fact proxy for the making of decisions relating to my health care in my place; and it is my intention that this appointment shall be honored by him/her, by my family, relatives, friends, physicians and lawyer as the final expression of my legal right to refuse medical or surgical treatment; and I accept the consequences of such a decision. I have duly executed a Durable Power of Attorney for health care decisions on this date.

3. In the absence of my ability to give further directions regarding my treatment, including life-sustaining procedures, it is my intention that this directive shall be honored by my family and physicians as the final expression of my legal right to refuse or accept medical and surgical treatment, and I accept the consequences of such refusal.

4. If I have been diagnosed as pregnant and that diagnosis is known to any interested person, this directive shall have no force during the course of my pregnancy.

5. I understand the full importance of this directive and am emotionally and mentally competent to make this directive. No participant in the making of this directive or in its being carried into effect, whether it be a medical doctor, my spouse, a relative, friend or any other person shall be held responsible in any way, legally, professionally or socially, for complying with my directions.

Signed _____

City, county and state of residence _____

The declarant has been known to me personally and I believe him/her to be of sound mind.

Witness _____ Witness _____

Address _____ Address _____

County of _____

State of _____

Before me, the undersigned authority, personally appeared _____,
_____, and _____
known to me to be Declarant and the Witnesses whose names are signed to the foregoing instrument, and who, in the
presence of each other, did subscribe their names to the Declaration on this date.

My commission expires:

_____
Notary Public

[Seal]

DECLARATION

If I should have an incurable or irreversible condition that will cause my death within a relatively short time, it is my desire that my life not be prolonged by administration of life-sustaining procedures. If my condition is terminal and I am unable to participate in decisions regarding my medical treatment, I direct my attending physician to withhold or withdraw procedures that merely prolong the dying process and are not necessary to my comfort or freedom from pain.

Signed this _____ day of _____, _____.

Signature _____

City, County and State and Residence _____

The declarant is known to me and voluntarily signed this document in my presence.

Witness _____

Address _____

Witness _____

Address _____

County of _____

State of _____

Before me, the undersigned authority, personally appeared _____,

_____, and _____

known to me to be Declarant and the Witnesses whose names are signed to the foregoing instrument, and who, in the presence of each other, did subscribe their names to the Declaration on this date.

My commission expires:

_____
Notary Public

[Seal]

Form #13

DECLARATION

Declaration made this _____ day of _____, _____. (month, year).

I, _____, willfully and voluntarily make known my desire that my dying shall not be artificially prolonged under the circumstances set forth below, and do hereby declare:

If at any time I should have a terminal condition and my attending and one (1) other physician in their discretion, have determined such condition is incurable and irreversible and will result in death within a relatively short time, and where the application of life-prolonging treatment would serve only to artificially prolong the dying process, I direct that such treatment be withheld or withdrawn, and that I be permitted to die naturally with only the administration of medication or the performance of any medical treatment deemed necessary to alleviate pain or for nutrition or hydration.

In the absence of my ability to give directions regarding the use of such life-prolonging treatment, it is my intention that this declaration shall be honored by my attending physician and my family as the final expression of my legal right to refuse medical or surgical treatment and I accept the consequences of such refusal.

If I have been diagnosed as pregnant and that diagnosis is known to my attending physician, this directive shall have no force or effect during the course of my pregnancy.

I understand the full import of this declaration and I am emotionally and mentally competent to make this declaration.

STATE OF KENTUCKY)
)Sct.

COUNTY OF _____)

Before me, the undersigned authority, on this day personally appeared _____,

Living Will Declarant, and _____, and _____

known to me to be witnesses whose names are each signed to the foregoing instrument, and all these persons being first

duly sworn, _____, Living Will Declarant, declared to me and to the witnesses in my presence that the instrument is the Living Will Declaration of the declarant and that the declarant has willingly signed and that such declarant executed it as a free and voluntary act for the purposes therein expressed; and each of the witnesses stated to me, in the presence and hearing of the Living Will Declarant, that the declarant signed the declaration as witness and to the best of such witness's knowledge, the Living Will Declarant was eighteen (18) years of age or over, of sound mind and under no constraint or undue influence.

_____
Living Will Declarant

_____
Address

_____
Witness

_____
Address

_____
Witness

_____
Address

Subscribed, sworn to and acknowledged before me by _____

_____, Living Will Declarant, and subscribed and sworn before

me by _____ and _____,

witnesses, on this the _____ day of _____ (year).

_____
Notary Public State At Large

_____
Date my commission expires

Form #14

DECLARATION

If I should have an incurable or irreversible condition that will cause my death within a short time, and if I am unable to participate in decisions regarding my medical treatment, I direct my attending physician to withhold or withdraw procedures that merely prolong the dying process and are not necessary to my comfort or freedom from pain.

Signed this _____ day of _____

  date   month   year

Signature _____

City, County and State of Residence _____

                                            city   county   state

The declarant is known to me and voluntarily signed this document in my presence.

Witness _____

Address _____

_____

Witness _____

Address _____

_____

County of _____

State of _____

Before me, the undersigned authority, personally appeared _____,

_____, and _____

known to me to be Declarant and the Witnesses whose names are signed to the foregoing instrument, and who, in the presence of each other, did subscribe their names to the Declaration on this date.

My commission expires:

_____

Notary Public

[Seal]

DECLARATION

On this _____ day of _____ (month, year), I, _____, being of sound mind, willfully and voluntarily direct that my dying shall not be artificially prolonged under the circumstances set forth in this declaration:

If at any time I should have an incurable injury, disease, or illness certified to be a terminal condition by two (2) physicians who have personally examined me, one (1) of whom shall be my attending physician, and the physicians have determined that my death is imminent and will occur whether or not life-sustaining procedures are utilized and where the application of such procedures would serve only to artificially prolong the dying process, I direct that such procedures be withheld or withdrawn, and that I be permitted to die naturally with only the administration of medication, the administration of food and water, and the performance of any medical procedure that is necessary to provide comfort care or alleviate pain. In the absence of my ability to give directions regarding the use of such life-sustaining procedures, it is my intention that this declaration shall be honored by my family and physician(s) as the final expression of my right to control my medical care and treatment.

I am legally competent to make this declaration, and I understand its full import.

Signed _____

Address _____

_____

Under penalty of perjury, we state that this declaration was signed by _____ in the presence of the undersigned who, at _____ request, in _____ presence, and in the presence of each other, have hereunto signed our names as witnesses this _____ day of _____ 19 _____.
Further, each of us, individually, states that: The declarant is known to me, and I believe the declarant to be of sound mind. I did not sign the declarant's signature to this declaration. Based upon information and belief, I am not related to the declarant by blood or marriage, a creditor of the declarant, entitled to any portion of the estate of the declarant under any existing testamentary instrument of the declarant, entitled to any financial benefit by reason of the death of the declarant, financially or otherwise responsible for the declarant's medical care, nor an employee of any such person or institution.

_____ Address _____

_____ Address _____

County of _____

State of _____

Before me, the undersigned authority, personally appeared _____, _____, and _____ known to me to be Declarant and the Witnesses whose names are signed to the foregoing instrument, and who, in the presence of each other, did subscribe their names to the Declaration on this date.

My commission expires:

_____
Notary Public

[Seal]

HEALTH CARE DECLARATION

Notice:

This is an important legal document. Before signing this document, you should know these important facts:

(a) This document gives your health care providers or your designated proxy the power and guidance to make health care decisions according to your wishes when you are in a terminal condition and cannot do so. This document may include what kind of treatment you want or do not want and under what circumstances you want these decisions to be made. You may state where you want or do not want to receive any treatment.

(b) If you name a proxy in this document and that person agrees to serve as your proxy, that person has a duty to act consistently with your wishes. If the proxy does not know your wishes, the proxy has the duty to act in your best interests. If you do not name a proxy, your health care providers have a duty to act consistently with your instructions or tell you that they are unwilling to do so.

(c) This document will remain valid and in effect until and unless you amend or revoke it. Review this document periodically to make sure it continues to reflect your preferences. You may amend or revoke the declaration at any time by notifying your health care providers.

(d) Your named proxy has the same right as you have to examine your medical records and to consent to their disclosure for purposes related to your health care or insurance unless you limit this right in this document.

(e) If there is anything in this document that you do not understand, you should ask for professional help to have it explained to you.

TO MY FAMILY, DOCTORS, AND ALL THOSE CONCERNED WITH MY CARE:

I, _____, being an adult of sound mind, willfully and voluntarily make this statement as a directive to be followed if I am in a terminal condition and become unable to participate in decisions regarding my health care. I understand that my health care providers are legally bound to act consistently with my wishes, within the limits of reasonable medical practice and other applicable law. I also understand that I have the right to make medical and health care decisions for myself as long as I am able to do so and to revoke this declaration at any time.

(1) The following are my feelings and wishes regarding my health care (you may state the circumstances under which this declaration applies):

(2) I particularly want to have all appropriate health care that will help in the following ways (you may give instructions for care you do want):

(3) I particularly do not want the following (you may list specific treatment you do not want in certain circumstances):

(4) I particularly want to have the following kinds of life-sustaining treatment if I am diagnosed to have a terminal condition (you may list the specific types of life-sustaining treatment that you do want if you have a terminal condition):

(5) I particularly do not want the following kinds of life-sustaining treatment if I am diagnosed to have a terminal condition (you may list the specific types of life-sustaining treatment that you do not want if you have a terminal condition):

Form #17

(6) I recognize that if I reject artificially administered sustenance, then I may die of dehydration or malnutrition rather than from my illness or injury. The following are my feelings and wishes regarding artificially administered sustenance should I have a terminal condition (you may indicate whether you wish to receive food and fluids given to you in some other way than by mouth if you have a terminal condition):

(7) Thoughts I feel are relevant to my instructions. (You may, but need not, give your religious beliefs, philosophy, or other personal values that you feel are important. You may also state preferences concerning the location of your care.)

(8) Proxy Designation. (If you wish, you may name someone to see that your wishes are carried out, but you do not have to do this. You may also name a proxy without including specific instructions regarding your care. If you name a proxy, you should discuss your wishes with that person.

If I become unable to communicate my instructions, I designate the following person(s) to act on my behalf consistently with my instructions, if any, as stated in this document. Unless I write instructions that limit my proxy's authority, my proxy has full power and authority to make health care decisions for me. If a guardian or conservator of the person is to be appointed for me, I nominate my proxy named in this document to act as guardian or conservator of my person.

Name: _____

Address: _____

Phone Number: _____

Relationship (If any): _____

If the person I have named above refuses or is unable or unavailable to act on my behalf, or if I revoke that person's authority to act as my proxy, I authorize the following person to do so:

Name: _____

Address: _____

Phone Number: _____

Relationship (If any): _____

I understand that I have the right to revoke the appointment of the persons named above to act on my behalf at any time by communicating that decision to the proxy or my health care provider.

DATE: _____

SIGNED: _____

STATE OF _____

COUNTY OF _____

Subscribed, sworn to, and acknowledged before me by _____

on this _____ day of _____, 19_____

_____

Notary Public
OR
(Sign and date here in the presence of two adult witnesses, neither of whom is entitled to any part of your estate under a will or by operation of law, and neither of whom is your proxy.)

I certify that the declarant voluntarily signed this declaration in my presence and that the declarant is personally known to me. I am not named as a proxy by the declaration, and to the best of my knowledge, I am not entitled to any part of the estate of the declarant under a will or by operation of law.

Witness _____ Address _____

Witness _____ Address _____

page 2 of 2

DECLARATION

DECLARATION made on _____ by _____
                      (date)   (person's name)

of _____, _____.
                                 (address)   (Social Security Number)

I, _____, being of sound mind, declare that if at any time I should suffer a terminal physical condition which causes me severe distress or unconsciousness, and my physician, with the concurrence of two (2) other physicians, believes that there is no expectation of my regaining consciousness or a state of health that is meaningful to me and but for the use of life-sustaining mechanisms my death would be imminent, I desire that the mechanisms be withdrawn so that I may die naturally. However, if I have been diagnosed as pregnant and that diagnosis is known to my physician, this declaration shall have no force or effect during the course of my pregnancy. I further declare that this declaration shall be honored by my family and my physician as the final expression of my desires concerning the manner in which I die.

SIGNED _____

I hereby witness this declaration and attest that:

(1) I personally know the Declarant and believe the Declarant to be of sound mind.

(2) To the best of my knowledge, at the time of the execution of this declaration, I:

(a) Am not related to the Declarant by blood or marriage,

(b) Do not have any claim on the estate of the Declarant,

(c) Am not entitled to any portion of the Declarant's estate by any will or by operation of law, and

(d) Am not a physician attending the Declarant or a person employed by a physician attending the Declarant.

WITNESS _____

ADDRESS _____

SOCIAL SECURITY NUMBER _____

WITNESS _____

ADDRESS _____

SOCIAL SECURITY NUMBER _____

County of _____

State of _____

Before me, the undersigned authority, personally appeared _____,

_____, and _____ known to me to be Declarant and the Witnesses whose names are signed to the foregoing instrument, and who, in the presence of each other, did subscribe their names to the Declaration on this date.

My commission expires:

_____
Notary Public

[Seal]

DECLARATION

I have the primary right to make my own decisions concerning treatment that might unduly prolong the dying process. By this declaration I express to my physician, family and friends my intent. If I should have a terminal condition it is my desire that my dying not be prolonged by administration of death-prolonging procedures. If my condition is terminal and I am unable to participate in decisions regarding my medical treatment, I direct my attending physician to withhold or withdraw medical procedures that merely prolong the dying process and are not necessary to my comfort or to alleviate pain. It is not my intent to authorize affirmative or deliberate acts or omissions to shorten my life rather only to permit the natural process of dying.

Signed this _____ day of _____

Signature _____

City, County and State of residence _____

The declarant is known to me, is eighteen years of age or older, of sound mind and voluntarily signed this document in my presence.

Witness _____

Address _____

Witness _____

Address _____

County of _____

State of _____

Before me, the undersigned authority, personally appeared _____,

_____, and _____

known to me to be Declarant and the Witnesses whose names are signed to the foregoing instrument, and who, in the presence of each other, did subscribe their names to the Declaration on this date.

My commission expires:

_____
Notary Public

[Seal]

REVOCATION PROVISION

I hereby revoke the above declaration.　　Signed _____
(Signature of Declarant)

Date _____

Form #19

DECLARATION

If I should have an incurable or irreversible condition that will cause my death within a relatively short time, it is my desire that my life not be prolonged by administration of life-sustaining procedures. If my condition is terminal and I am unable to participate in decisions regarding my medical treatment, I direct my attending physician to withhold or withdraw procedures that merely prolong the dying process and are not necessary to my comfort or freedom from pain. It is my intention that this declaration shall be valid until revoked by me.

Signed this _____ day of _____

Signature _____

City, County, and State of Residence _____

The declarant is known to me and voluntarily signed this document in my presence.

Witness _____

Address _____

Witness _____

Address _____

County of _____

State of _____

Before me, the undersigned authority, personally appeared _____,

_____, and _____

known to me to be Declarant and the Witnesses whose names are signed to the foregoing instrument, and who, in the presence of each other, did subscribe their names to the Declaration on this date.

My commission expires:

_____

Notary Public

[Seal]

Form #20

DIRECTIVE TO PHYSICIANS

Date _____

I, _____, being of sound mind, intentionally and voluntarily declare:

1. If at any time I am in a terminal condition and become comatose or am otherwise rendered incapable of communicating with my attending physician, and my death is imminent because of an incurable disease, illness or injury, I direct that life-sustaining procedures be withheld or withdrawn, and that I be permitted to die naturally.

2. It is my intention that this directive be honored by my family and attending physician as the final expression of my legal right to refuse medical or surgical treatment and to accept the consequences of my refusal.

3. If I have been found to be pregnant, and that fact is known to my physician, this directive is void during the course of my pregnancy. I understand the full import of this directive, and I am emotionally and mentally competent to execute it.

Signed _____

City, County and State of Residence _____

The declarant has been personally known to me and I believe _____ to be of sound mind.

Witness _____

Witness _____

County of _____

State of _____

Before me, the undersigned authority, personally appeared _____, _____, and _____

known to me to be Declarant and the Witnesses whose names are signed to the foregoing instrument, and who, in the presence of each other, did subscribe their names to the Declaration on this date.

My commission expires:

_____
Notary Public

[Seal]

Form #21

DECLARATION OF A DESIRE FOR A NATURAL DEATH

I, _____, being of sound mind, desire that my life not be prolonged by extraordinary means if my condition is determined to be terminal and incurable. I am aware and understand that this writing authorizes a physician to withhold or discontinue extraordinary means.

This the _____ day of _____

Signature _____

I hereby state that the declarant, _____, being of sound mind signed the above declaration in my presence and that I am not related to the declarant by blood or marriage and that I do not know or have a reasonable expectation that I would be entitled to any portion of the estate of the declarant under any existing will or codicil of the declarant or as an heir under the Intestate Succession Act if the declarant died on this date without a will. I also state that I am not the declarant's attending physician or an employee of the declarant's attending physician, or an employee of a health facility in which the declarant is a patient or an employee of a nursing home or any group-care home where the declarant resides. I further state that I do not now have any claim against the declarant.

Witness _____

Witness _____

The clerk or the assistant clerk, or a notary public may, upon proper proof, certify the declaration as follows:

Certificate

I, _____, Clerk (Assistant Clerk) of Superior Court or Notary Public (circle one as appropriate) for _____ County hereby certify that _____, the declarant, appeared before me and swore to me and to the witnesses in my presence that this instrument is his Declaration Of A Desire For A Natural Death, and that he had willingly and voluntarily made and executed it as his free act and deed for the purposes expressed in it.

I further certify that _____ and _____, witnesses, appeared before me and swore that they witnessed _____, declarant, sign the attached declaration, believing him to be of sound mind; and also swore that at the time they witnessed the declaration (i) they were not related within the third degree to the declarant or to the declarant's spouse, and (ii) they did not know or have a reasonable expectation that they would be entitled to any portion of the estate of the declarant upon the declarant's death under any will of the declarant or codicil thereto then existing or under the Intestate Succession Act as it provides at that time, and (iii) they were not a physician attending the declarant or an employee of an attending physician or an employee of a health facility in which the declarant was a patient or an employee of a nursing home or any group-care home in which the declarant resided, and (iv) they did not have a claim against the declarant. I further certify that I am satisfied as to the genuineness and due execution of the declaration.

This the _____ day of _____

Clerk (Assistant Clerk) of Superior Court or Notary Public (circle one as appropriate) for the County of _____

_____, State of _____

Form #22

DIRECTIVE TO PHYSICIANS

Directive made this _____ day of _____ (month, year).

I, _____, being of sound mind and twenty-one (21) years of age or older, willfully and voluntarily make known my desire that my life shall not be artificially prolonged under the circumstances set forth below, and do hereby declare:

    1. If at any time I should have an incurable irreversible condition caused by injury, disease, or illness certified to be a terminal condition by two physicians, I direct that life-sustaining procedures be withheld or withdrawn and that I be permitted to die naturally, if the application of life-sustaining procedures would serve only to artificially prolong the moment of my death and my attending physician determines that my death is imminent whether or not life-sustaining procedures are utilized;

    2. In the absence of my ability to give directions regarding the use of such life-sustaining procedures, it is my intention that this directive shall be honored by my family and physicians as the final expression of my legal right to refuse medical or surgical treatment and accept the consequences of such refusal;

    3. If I have been diagnosed as pregnant and that diagnosis is known to my physician, this directive shall have no force or effect during the course of my pregnancy;

    4. I have been diagnosed and notified as having a terminal condition by _____, M.D. or D.O., whose address is _____, and whose telephone number is _____.

I understand that if I have not filled in the name and address of the physician, it shall be presumed that I did not have a terminal condition when I made out this directive;

    5. This directive shall be in effect until it is revoked;

    6. I understand the full import of this directive and I am emotionally and mentally competent to make this directive; and

    7. I understand that I may revoke this directive at any time.

                                 Signed _____

City, County and State of Residence _____

The declarant has been personally known to me and I believe said declarant to be of sound mind. I am twenty-one (21) years of age or older, I am not related to the declarant by blood or marriage, nor would I be entitled to any portion of the estate of the declarant upon the death of said declarant, nor am I the attending physician of the declarant or an employee of the attending physician or a health care facility in which the declarant is a patient, or a patient in the health care facility in which the declarant is a patient, nor am I financially responsible for the medical care of the declarant, or any person who has a claim against any portion of the estate of the declarant upon the death of the declarant.

                              Witness _____

                              Witness _____

State of Oklahoma

County of _____

Before me, the undersigned authority, on this day personally appeared _____,

                                          (declarant)

_____, and _____ whose names are
       (witness)   (witness)

subscribed to the foregoing instrument in their respective capacities, and, all of said persons being by me duly sworn, the declarant declared to me and to the said witnesses in my presence that said instrument is his or her "Directive to Physicians," and that the declarant had willingly and voluntarily made and executed it as the free act and deed of the declarant for the purposes therein expressed.

The foregoing instrument was acknowledged before me this _____ day of _____, 19 _____

Signed _____

Notary Public in and for _____ County, State of _____

Form #23

DIRECTIVE TO PHYSICIANS

Directive made this _____ day of _____ (month, year).

I _____, being of sound mind, willfully and voluntarily make known my desire that my life shall not be artificially prolonged under the circumstances set forth below and do hereby declare:

1. If at any time I should have an incurable injury, disease or illness certified to be a terminal condition by two physicians, one of whom is the attending physician, and where the application of life-sustaining procedures would serve only to artificially prolong the moment of my death and where my physician determines that my death is imminent whether or not life-sustaining procedures are utilized, I direct that such procedures be withheld or withdrawn, and that I be permitted to die naturally.

2. In the absence of my ability to give directions regarding the use of such life-sustaining procedures, it is my intention that this directive shall be honored by my family and physician(s) as the final expression of my legal right to refuse medical or surgical treatment and accept the consequences from such refusal.

3. I understand the full import of this directive and I am emotionally and mentally competent to make this directive.

Signed _____

City, County and State of Residence _____

I hereby witness this directive and attest that:

    (1) I personally know the Declarant and believe the Declarant to be of sound mind.

    (2) To the best of my knowledge, at the time of the execution of this directive, I:

    (a) Am not related to the Declarant by blood or marriage,

    (b) Do not have any claim on the estate of the Declarant,

    (c) Am not entitled to any portion of the Declarant's estate by any will or by operation of law, and

    (d) Am not a physician attending the Declarant, a person employed by a physician attending the Declarant or a person employed by a health facility in which the Declarant is a patient.

    (3) I understand that if I have not witnessed this directive in good faith I may be responsible for any damages that arise out of giving this directive its intended effect.

Witness _____

Witness _____

County of _____

State of _____

Before me, the undersigned authority, personally appeared _____,

_____, and _____

known to me to be Declarant and the Witnesses whose names are signed to the foregoing instrument, and who, in the presence of each other, did subscribe their names to the Declaration on this date.

My commission expires:

_____

Notary Public

[Seal]

STATE OF SOUTH CAROLINA
DECLARATION OF A DESIRE FOR A NATURAL DEATH
COUNTY OF _____

I, _____, being at least eighteen years of age and a

resident of and domiciled in the City of _____, County of _____,

State of South Carolina, make this Declaration this _____ day of _____, 19_____.

I willfully and voluntarily make known my desire that no life-sustaining procedures be used to prolong my dying if my condition is terminal, and I declare:

If at any time I have a condition certified to be a terminal condition by two physicians who have personally examined me, one of whom is my attending physician, and the physicians have determined that my death will occur within a relatively short period of time without the use of life-sustaining procedures and where the application of life-sustaining procedures would serve only to prolong the dying process, I direct that the procedures be withheld or withdrawn, and that I be permitted to die naturally with only the administration of medication or the performance of any medical procedure necessary to provide me with comfort care.

In the absence of my ability to give directions regarding the use of life-sustaining procedures, it is my intention that this Declaration be honored by my family and physicians and any health facility in which I may be a patient as the final expression of my legal right to refuse medical or surgical treatment, and I accept the consequences from the refusal.

I am aware that this Declaration authorizes a physician to withhold or withdraw life-sustaining procedures. I am emotionally and mentally competent to make this Declaration.

THIS DECLARATION MAY BE REVOKED:

(1) BY BEING DEFACED, TORN, OBLITERATED, OR OTHERWISE DESTROYED, IN EXPRESSION OF THE DECLARANT'S INTENT TO REVOKE, BY THE DECLARANT OR BY SOME PERSON IN THE PRESENCE OF AND BY THE DIRECTION OF THE DECLARANT. REVOCATION BY DESTRUCTION OF ONE OR MORE OF MULTIPLE ORIGINAL DECLARATIONS REVOKES ALL OF THE ORIGINAL DECLARATIONS. THE REVOCATION OF THE ORIGINAL DECLARATIONS ACTUALLY NOT DESTROYED BECOMES EFFECTIVE ONLY UPON COMMUNICATION TO THE ATTENDING PHYSICIAN. THE ATTENDING PHYSICIAN SHALL RECORD IN THE DECLARANT'S MEDICAL RECORD THE TIME AND DATE WHEN THE PHYSICIAN RECEIVED NOTIFICATION OF THE REVOCATION;

(2) BY A WRITTEN REVOCATION SIGNED AND DATED BY THE DECLARANT EXPRESSING HIS INTENT TO REVOKE. THE REVOCATION BECOMES EFFECTIVE ONLY UPON COMMUNICATION TO THE ATTENDING PHYSICIAN. THE ATTENDING PHYSICIAN SHALL RECORD IN THE DECLARANT'S MEDICAL RECORD THE TIME AND DATE WHEN THE PHYSICIAN RECEIVED NOTIFICATION OF THE WRITTEN REVOCATION;

(3) BY AN ORAL EXPRESSION BY THE DECLARANT OF HIS INTENT TO REVOKE THE DECLARATION. THE REVOCATION BECOMES EFFECTIVE ONLY UPON COMMUNICATION TO THE ATTENDING PHYSICIAN BY THE DECLARANT. HOWEVER, AN ORAL REVOCATION MADE BY THE DECLARANT BECOMES EFFECTIVE UPON COMMUNICATION TO THE ATTENDING PHYSICIAN BY A PERSON OTHER THAN THE DECLARANT IF:

(a) THE PERSON WAS PRESENT WHEN THE ORAL REVOCATION WAS MADE;
(b) THE REVOCATION WAS COMMUNICATED TO THE PHYSICIAN WITHIN A REASONABLE TIME;
(c) THE PHYSICAL OR MENTAL CONDITION OF THE DECLARANT MAKES IT IMPOSSIBLE FOR THE PHYSICIAN TO CONFIRM THROUGH SUBSEQUENT CONVERSATION WITH THE DECLARANT THAT THE REVOCATION HAS OCCURRED.

THE ATTENDING PHYSICIAN SHALL RECORD IN THE PATIENT'S MEDICAL RECORD THE TIME, DATE, AND PLACE OF THE REVOCATION AND THE TIME, DATE, AND PLACE, IF DIFFERENT, OR WHEN HE RECEIVED NOTIFICATION OF THE REVOCATION. TO BE EFFECTIVE AS A REVOCATION, THE ORAL EXPRESSION CLEARLY MUST INDICATE A DESIRE THAT THE DECLARATION NOT BE GIVEN EFFECT OR THAT LIFE-SUSTAINING PROCEDURES BE ADMINISTERED;

(4) BY A WRITTEN, SIGNED, AND DATED REVOCATION OR AN ORAL REVOCATION BY A PERSON DESIGNATED BY THE DECLARANT IN THE DECLARATION, EXPRESSING THE DESIGNEE'S INTENT PERMANENTLY OR TEMPORARILY TO REVOKE THE DECLARATION. THE REVOCATION BECOMES EFFECTIVE ONLY UPON COMMUNICATION TO THE ATTENDING PHYSICIAN BY THE DESIGNEE. THE ATTENDING PHYSICIAN SHALL RECORD IN THE DECLARANT'S MEDICAL RECORD THE TIME, DATE, AND PLACE OF THE REVOCATION AND THE TIME, DATE, AND PLACE, IF DIFFERENT, OF WHEN THE PHYSICIAN

RECEIVED NOTIFICATION OF THE REVOCATION. A DESIGNEE MAY REVOKE ONLY IF THE DECLARANT IS INCOMPETENT TO DO SO. IF THE DECLARANT WISHES TO DESIGNATE A PERSON WITH AUTHORITY TO REVOKE THIS DECLARATION ON HIS BEHALF, THE NAME AND ADDRESS OF THAT PERSON MUST BE ENTERED BELOW: THIS DECLARATION ON HIS BEHALF, THE NAME AND ADDRESS OF THAT PERSON MUST BE ENTERED BELOW:

_____   _____

NAME OF DESIGNEE

                                             _____
                                             ADDRESS

_____
Declarant

AFFIDAVIT

STATE OF _____

COUNTY OF _____

We, _____ and _____, the undersigned

witnesses to the foregoing Declaration, dated the _____ day of _____,

19_____, being first duly sworn, declare to the undersigned authority, on the basis of our best information and belief, that the Declaration was on that date signed by the declarant as and for his DECLARATION OF A DESIRE FOR A NATURAL DEATH in our presence and we, at his request and in his presence, and in the presence of each other, subscribe our names as witnesses on that date. The declarant is personally known to us, and we believe him to be of sound mind. Each of us affirms that he is qualified as a witness to this Declaration under the provisions of the South Carolina Death With Dignity Act in that he is not related to the declarant by blood or marriage, either as a spouse, lineal ancestor, descendant of the parents of the declarant, or spouse of any of them; nor directly financially responsible for the declarant's medical care; nor entitled to any portion of the declarant's estate upon his decease, whether under any will or as an heir by intestate succession; nor the beneficiary of a life insurance policy of the declarant; nor the declarant's attending physician; nor an employee of the attending physician; nor a person who has a claim against the declarant's decedent's estate as of this time. No more than one of us is an employee of a health facility in which the declarant is a patient. If the declarant is a patient in a hospital or skilled or intermediate care nursing facility at the date of execution of this Declaration at least one of us is an ombudsman designated by the State Ombudsman, Office of the Governor.

_____
Witness

_____
Witness

Subscribed before me by _____, the declarant, and subscribed and sworn

to before me by _____ and _____,

the witnesses, this _____ day of _____, 19_____.

Notary Public for _____

My commission expires: _____

[Seal]

page 2 of 2

DIRECTIVE TO PHYSICIANS AND PROVIDERS OF MEDICAL SERVICES

(Pursuant to Section 75-2-1104, UCA)

This directive is made this _____ day of _____, _____.

1. I, _____, being of sound mind, willfully and voluntarily make known my desire that my life not be artificially prolonged by life-sustaining procedures except as I may otherwise provide in this directive.

2. I declare that if at any time I should have an injury, disease, or illness, which is certified in writing to be a terminal condition by two physicians who have personally examined me, and in the opinion of those physicians the application of life-sustaining procedures would serve only to unnaturally prolong the moment of my death and to unnaturally postpone or prolong the dying process, I direct that these procedures be withheld or withdrawn and my death be permitted to occur naturally.

3. I expressly intend this directive to be a final expression of my legal right to refuse medical or surgical treatment and to accept the consequences from this refusal which shall remain in effect notwithstanding my future inability to give current medical directions to treating physicians and other providers of medical services.

4. I understand that the term "life-sustaining procedure" does not include the administration of medication or sustenance, or the performance of any medical procedure deemed necessary to provide comfort care, or to alleviate pain, except to the extent I specify below that any of these procedures be considered life-sustaining.

5. I reserve the right to give current medical directions to physicians and other providers of medical services so long as I am able, even though these directions may conflict with the above written directive that life-sustaining procedures be withheld or withdrawn.

6. I understand the full import of this directive and declare that I am emotionally and mentally competent to make this directive.

_____ Declarant's signature

_____

City, County, and State of Residence

We witnesses certify that each of us is 18 years of age or older and each personally witnessed the declarant sign or direct the signing of this directive; that we are acquainted with the declarant and believe him to be of sound mind; that the declarant's desires are as expressed above; that neither of us is a person who signed the above directive on behalf of the declarant; that we are not related to the declarant by blood or marriage nor are we entitled to any portion of declarant's estate according to the laws of intestate succession of this state or under any will or codicil of declarant; that we are not directly financially responsible for declarant's medical care; and that we are not agents of any health care facility in which the declarant may be a patient at the time of signing this directive.

_____	_____
Signature of Witness	Signature of Witness
_____	_____
Address of Witness	Address of Witness

County of _____

State of _____

Before me, the undersigned authority, personally appeared _____,

_____, and _____

known to me to be Declarant and the Witnesses whose names are signed to the foregoing instrument, and who, in the presence of each other, did subscribe their names to the Declaration on this date.

My commission expires:

_____

Notary Public

[Seal]

Form #26

DECLARATION

To my family, my physician, my lawyer, my clergyman. To any medical facility in whose care I happen to be. To any individual who may become responsible for my health, welfare or affairs.

Death is as much a reality as birth, growth, maturity and old age—it is the one certainty of life. If the time comes when I, _____, can no longer take part in decisions of my own future, let this statement stand as an expression of my wishes, while I am still of sound mind.

If the situation should arise in which I am in a terminal state and there is no reasonable expectation of my recovery, I direct that I be allowed to die a natural death and that my life not be prolonged by extraordinary measures. I do, however, ask that medication be mercifully administered to me to alleviate suffering even though this may shorten my remaining life.

This statement is made after careful consideration and is in accordance with my strong convictions and beliefs. I want the wishes and directions here expressed carried out to the extent permitted by law. Insofar as they are not legally enforceable, I hope that those to whom this will is addressed will regard themselves as morally bound by these provisions.

Signed: _____

Date: _____

Witness: _____

Witness: _____

Copies of this request have been given to:

_____

_____

County of _____

State of _____

Before me, the undersigned authority, personally appeared _____, _____, and _____ known to me to be Declarant and the Witnesses whose names are signed to the foregoing instrument, and who, in the presence of each other, did subscribe their names to the Declaration on this date.

My commission expires:

_____
Notary Public

[Seal]

DIRECTIVE TO PHYSICIANS

Directive made this _____ day of _____ (month, year).

I _____, being of sound mind, willfully, and voluntarily make known my desire that my life shall not be artificially prolonged under the circumstances set forth below, and do hereby declare that:

(a) If at any time I should have an incurable injury, disease, or illness certified to be a terminal condition by two physicians, and where the application of life-sustaining procedures would serve only to artificially prolong the moment of my death and where my physician determines that my death is imminent whether or not life-sustaining procedures are utilized, I direct that such procedures be withheld or withdrawn, and that I be permitted to die naturally.

(b) In the absence of my ability to give directions regarding the use of such life-sustaining procedures, it is my intention that this directive shall be honored by my family and physician(s) as the final expression of my legal right to refuse medical or surgical treatment and I accept the consequences from such refusal.

(c) If I have been diagnosed as pregnant and that diagnosis is known to my physician, this directive shall have no force or effect during the course of my pregnancy.

(d) I understand the full import of this directive and I am emotionally and mentally competent to make this directive.

Signed _____

City, County, and State of Residence _____

The declarer has been personally known to me and I believe him or her to be of sound mind.

Witness _____

Witness _____

County of _____

State of _____

Before me, the undersigned authority, personally appeared _____,

_____, and _____

known to me to be Declarant and the Witnesses whose names are signed to the foregoing instrument, and who, in the presence of each other, did subscribe their names to the Declaration on this date.

My commission expires:

_____
Notary Public

[Seal]

Form #28

DECLARATION TO PHYSICIANS

Declaration made this _____ day of _____ (month), _____ (year).

1. I, _____, being of sound mind, willfully and voluntarily state my desire that my dying may not be artificially prolonged if I have an incurable injury or illness certified to be a terminal condition by 2 physicians who have personally examined me, one of whom is my attending physician, and if the physicians have determined that my death is imminent, so that the application of life-sustaining procedures would serve only to prolong artificially the dying process. Under these circumstances, I direct that life-sustaining procedures be withheld or withdrawn and that I be permitted to die naturally, with only:

  a. The continuation of nutritional support and fluid maintenance; and

  b. The alleviation of pain by administering medication or other medical procedure.

2. If I am unable to give directions regarding the use of life-sustaining procedures, I intend that my family and physician honor this declaration as the final expression of my legal right to refuse medical or surgical treatment and to accept the consequences from this refusal.

3. If I have been diagnosed as pregnant and my physician knows of this diagnosis, this declaration has no effect during the course of my pregnancy.

4. This declaration takes effect immediately.

I understand this declaration and I am emotionally and mentally competent to make this declaration.

Signed _____

Address _____

I know the declarant personally and I believe him or her to be of sound mind. I am not related to the declarant by blood or marriage, and am not entitled to any portion of the declarant's estate under any will of the declarant. I am neither the declarant's attending physician, the attending nurse, the attending medical staff nor an employee of the attending physician or of the inpatient health care facility in which the declarant may be a patient and I have no claim against the declarant's estate at this time, except that, if I am not a health care provider who is involved in the medical care of the declarant, I may be an employee of the inpatient health care facility regardless of whether or not the facility may have a claim against the estate of the declarant.

Witness _____

Witness _____

County of _____

State of _____

Before me, the undersigned authority, personally appeared _____,

_____, and _____ known to me to be Declarant and the Witnesses whose names are signed to the foregoing instrument, and who, in the presence of each other, did subscribe their names to the Declaration on this date.

My commission expires:

_____
Notary Public

[Seal]

Wyoming

DECLARATION

Declaration made this _____ day of _____ (month, year).

I, _____, being of sound mind, willfully and voluntarily make known my desire that my dying shall not be artificially prolonged under the circumstances set forth below, do hereby declare:

If at any time I should have an incurable injury, disease or other illness certified to be a terminal condition by two (2) physicians who have personally examined me, one (1) of whom shall be my attending physician, and the physicians have determined that my death will occur whether or not life-sustaining procedures are utilized and where the application of life-sustaining procedures would serve only to artificially prolong the dying process, I direct that such procedure be withheld or withdrawn, and that I be permitted to die naturally with only the administration of medication or the performance of any medical procedure deemed necessary to provide me with comfort care. If, in spite of this declaration, I am comatose or otherwise unable to make treatment decisions for myself, I HEREBY designate _____

_____ to make treatment decisions for me.

In the absence of my ability to give directions regarding the use of life-sustaining procedures, it is my intention that this declaration shall be honored by my family and physician(s) and agent as the final expression of my legal right to refuse medical or surgical treatment and accept the consequences from this refusal. I understand the full import of this declaration and I am emotionally and mentally competent to make this declaration.

Signed _____

City, County and State of Residence _____

_____

The declarant has been personally known to me and I believe him or her to be of sound mind. I did not sign the declarant's signature above for or at the direction of the declarant. I am not related to the declarant by blood or marriage, entitled to any portion of the estate of the declarant according to the laws of intestate succession under any will of the declarant or codicil thereto, or directly financially responsible for declarant's medical care.

Witness _____

Witness _____

County of _____

State of _____

Before me, the undersigned authority, personally appeared _____,

_____, and _____

known to me to be Declarant and the Witnesses whose names are signed to the foregoing instrument, and who, in the presence of each other, did subscribe their names to the Declaration on this date.

My commission expires:

_____
Notary Public

[Seal]

Form #30

GLOSSARY

acknowledgment: a formal validation of an act or document, as performed, for example, by a notary public

attending physician: the doctor who treats the maker of a Living Will

declarant: the maker of a Living Will

emancipated minor: a person who, although under the age of legal adulthood, is given by state law certain rights of an adult

execution: the procedure involving signing, witnessing, and notarizing a Living Will

filing requirements: whether a maker of a Living Will must give a copy of the executed Living Will to the treating physician for it to be effective

heir at law: a person who inherits the estate of one who dies without a Last Will and Testament

intestate succession: rules for inheritance of the estate of one who dies without a valid Last Will and Testament

notary: a person commissioned by the state to formally witness documents and execute acknowledgments

ombudsman: under certain state laws, someone licensed by the state to oversee various health care issues

revocation: the procedure by which a Living Will may be voided and nullified

statute: a law

third degree: a measure of family relationship. The following are related to you within the third degree or less: your parents, children, grandparents, grandchildren, brothers and sisters, uncles and aunts, nieces and nephews, great-grandparents.

treating physician: *see* **attending physician**

witness: one who, being present, personally acknowledges the signing of a document; an eyewitness

NOTES

NOTES